THE VIOLIN CONCERTO

Da Capo Press Music Reprint Series

GENERAL EDITOR

FREDERICK FREEDMAN

VASSAR COLLEGE

THE VIOLIN CONCERTO

A Study in German Romanticism

By Benjamin F. Swalin

DA CAPO PRESS • NEW YORK • 1973

Library of Congress Cataloging in Publication Data

Swalin, Benjamin Franklin, 1901-
  The violin concerto.

  (Da Capo Press music reprint series)
  Bibliography: p.
  1. Concerto (Violin)   2. Romanticism in music.   I. Title
ML856.S9V5   1973   785.6   72-8292
ISBN 0-306-70537-0

This Da Capo Press edition of *The Violin Concerto*
is an unabridged republication of the first edition
published in Chapel Hill, North Carolina, in 1941.
It is reprinted by special arrangement with the author.

Copyright, 1941, by The University of
North Carolina Press

Published by Da Capo Press, Inc.
A Subsidiary of Plenum Publishing Corporation
227 West 17th Street, New York, New York 10011

Manufactured in the United States of America

THE VIOLIN CONCERTO

THE

VIOLIN CONCERTO

A Study in German Romanticism

Benjamin F. Swalin, Ph.D.

CHAPEL HILL
The University of North Carolina Press
1941

THE PUBLICATION OF THIS VOLUME HAS BEEN AIDED
BY A GRANT FROM THE AMERICAN COUNCIL OF LEARNED SOCIETIES

PRINTED IN THE UNITED STATES OF AMERICA
BY THE WILLIAM BYRD PRESS, INC.
RICHMOND, VIRGINIA

TO THE MEMORY OF

MY MOTHER AND FATHER

PREFACE

I N THIS DISQUISITION on the violin concerto in German Romanticism we propose to consider the works which are representative of composers from Spohr to Brahms, embracing, approximately, the period from 1802 to 1885.[1]

We shall interest ourselves not only in the essential musical
qualities of a composer's style, but also in the particular technical
features that are characteristic and idiomatic. The question as to
whether or not the musical ideas are well conceived and adroitly
manipulated is a point on which there can be some reasonable
agreement; but whether or not a composition or even a theme can
be judged esthetically attractive and beautiful is a matter on which
eminent critics may differ egregiously. With this in mind, therefore, we essay the task of making a stylistic criticism.

Neither orchestra scores nor pianoforte and violin transcriptions
were available for some of the concertos discussed in Chapter III,
and it became necessary, therefore, to utilize separate orchestra
parts for some of the analyses.

The author desires to express his gratitude to the American

1. We exclude, however, the Beethoven Violin Concerto, opus 61, written in
1806, on the thesis that it is a Classical work culminating another era. See *infra*,
pp. 3, 6-7.

Council of Learned Societies for encouragement and assistance in connection with the publication of this work; to Professor Robert W. Lach and Professor Robert M. Haas, of the University of Vienna, for criticisms pertaining to the original manuscript; and to Professor Jan Philip Schinhan, of the University of North Carolina, for stimulating and helpful suggestions. The author likewise offers profound thanks to his wife for reading the manuscript and copying the musical examples.

CONTENTS

THE VIOLIN CONCERTO

INTRODUCTION

ALTHOUGH the origin of the violin concerto is not our specific problem, we are nevertheless committed to outline briefly its evolution and development up to and inclusive of Beethoven's work before we proceed with the discussion of the concerto during the Romantic period.

The art of violin playing, during the seventeenth century, attained through such virtuosi as Schop, Strungk, Baltzar, Walther, and Biber "... a highly independent and unique technical development marked by careful use of the positions, remarkable skill in the execution of double-stops, and a predilection for the *scordatura.*"[1] Substantial progress may be observed during the eighteenth century in the achievements of J. C. Stamitz, I. Fränzl, C. Cannabich, and the Eck brothers of the Mannheim School; and J. B. Graun and F. Benda of the Berlin School.

Highly significant in the development of violin technique was the publication of instruction books and violin studies. *The Art of Playing the Violin,* by Francesco Geminiani, appeared in 1740. About the same time, Pietro Locatelli wrote his *L'Arte di Nuova Modulazione,* opus 9, "... which did not have its merited success

1. R. M. Haas, *Aufführungspraxis der Musik* (Handbuch der Musikwissenschaft, hsg. von E. Bücken), p. 205.

because of its novelty and excessive difficulties, and perhaps also because of the fact that, when Locatelli published his work, the time had not yet arrived for a composer to depart from the Classical forms."[2] But his work became adumbrative of the important Paganini *Twenty-four Caprices* of the nineteenth century. Leopold Mozart's *Versuch einer gründlichen Violinschule* was published in 1756, and through its various editions and translations, became accessible to a large public.

In France, Giovanni Battista Viotti was significant ". . . not only because of his extraordinary ability as a violinist, but more especially because of his influence on composers of the time and the following epoch. . . ."[3] His successors, Rode, Kreutzer, and Baillot, exerted a potent influence on the Romantic composers of the violin concerto, and formulated the fundamental principles of modern violin playing in their *L'Art du Violon* (1834).

We do not observe a truly modern development of bowing technique until late in the eighteenth century, when François Tourte improved the construction of the violin bow. He chose wood of a fine but strong texture, and bent the stick the "reverse" way, establishing correct proportions of curvature, height, and length. From that time the art of bowing made remarkable progress, culminating in the unexcelled mastery of Paganini, Joachim, and Sarasate.

In the formal evolution of the solo violin concerto, Schering enumerates some of the outstanding personalities: Torelli, Vivaldi, J. S. Bach, Bonporti, Tartini, Giornovichi, Viotti, W. A. Mozart, and Beethoven.[4] It was Mozart, however, who provided the concerto model for the composers of the nineteenth century. His general plan embraced three movements.

2. F. J. Fétis, *Biographie Universelle des Musiciens* (deuxième édition, 1884), Vol. VI, p. 415.

3. J. Joachim and A. Moser, *Violinschule,* Vol. I, p. 191.

4. A. Schering, "Das Solo-Konzert," in *Geschichte des Instrumentalkonzerts,* Chap. III.

In Mozart's first movement, usually an Allegro, a sonata form with a double exposition was employed as the standard design.[5] A substantial orchestral exposition containing two contrasting themes in the tonic key was freely reproduced in a second exposition (solo exposition), in which both the solo instrument and the orchestra participated. Here the second theme was set forth in a related key, thus establishing a principle of key duality. A development section followed, with the orchestra and solo exploiting fragmentary thematic and harmonic manipulations in a wide gamut of tonalities, and occasionally introducing new and extraneous material. After a transition, there was a reprise (recapitulation) in which the material from the exposition was restated. Both themes, however, were presented in the tonic key so as to preserve a unity of tonality. Near the close of the movement there was a fermata on a tonic six-four, or dominant chord, after which a violin cadenza was generally introduced. If the cadenza were improvised or composed by the soloist, it was essential for him to display his skill in manipulating the significant musical ideas of the movement. He was also expected to impress his auditors with his technical dexterity. The cadenza frequently concluded with a long trill and diminuendo over a dominant chord, and was followed immediately by a brief coda. In the concertos of Mozart the coda merely served the purpose of making an effective conclusion.

For the middle movement, a rather ornate Adagio, Andante, or Larghetto was preferred. Its structure was usually that of a binary or ternary form, although Mozart occasionally applied broader and more complex designs.[6] The tonality was either the dominant or sub-dominant, until the Romanticists began to emphasize mediant, sub-mediant, and other key inter-relationships. The finale was a Rondo, "... ein heiteres, gefälliges Musikstück,

5. Cf. Mozart, Concerto for Violin and Orchestra in G major, K. 216.
6. The Adagio of Mozart's Concerto for Violin and Orchestra in B-flat major, K. 207, has an ingenious and cohesive design that eludes classification in terms of an orthodox and established form.

dessen Thema oder Anfangssatz öfters wiederkehrt."[7] According to Schering, this type of closing movement was first adapted to the violin concerto by Giornovichi, one of Mozart's contemporaries.[8]

Beethoven composed his epochal Concerto for Violin and Orchestra in D major, opus 61, during the year 1806.[9] In that work he amplified the achievements of Mozart by utilizing larger and more comprehensive designs and effecting a remarkable fusion of the solo violin and orchestra. The conception was symphonic and along the same lines that Brahms, seventy-two years later, conceived his Violin Concerto, opus 77.

Among the striking traits of the first movement (Allegro ma non troppo) are not only the significance of the orchestral part, but also the expansive proportions of the sonata form and the concentrative use of motive structures. The orchestral exposition contains statements of both themes in the tonic key, the second of which is promptly reiterated in the tonic minor key. The violin cadenza was left to the discretion of the soloist, and immediately preceded the brief but important coda.

The Larghetto, in the sub-dominant key(G), is a profound movement in which the solo violin frequently assumes the role of an embellishing obligato instrument. A kind of free variation form is used, and this may be analyzed in the following sections, each comprising a period: A — A^1 — A^2 — A — B — A^3 — B^1 — transition. The last section includes a cadenza (*ad libitum*) lead-

7. L. Spohr, *Violinschule* (Originalausgabe, 1832), p. 142.

8. A. Schering, *Geschichte des Instrumentalkonzerts*, p. 171.

9. The concerto was given its première in Vienna on December 23, 1806, with Franz Clement as soloist. Other early performances included those by

> L. Tomasini, Jr., 1812, Berlin
> Baillot, 1828, Paris
> Vieuxtemps, 1833, Vienna
> Uhlrich, 1836, Leipzig
> Joachim, 1844, London

The orchestra parts of the concerto were published in August, 1808.

ing into the Rondo. Similar devices for linking the movements of a concerto were appropriated by later composers.

The voluminous Rondo (Allegro) has the design: A — B — A — C — A — B — cadenza — coda. The organic unity of the movement and the virtuosic quality of the solo part are inherent technical virtues.

In order that we may view the evolution and progress of instrumentation with respect to the violin concerto, it is essential to refer again to Mozart. The accompaniments of his Concertos in G major (K. 216), D major (K. 218), and A major (K. 219) are scored for

> 2 oboes
> 2 horns
> strings

The wind instruments are entirely subservient to the strings. Beethoven, however, employed a larger orchestra in the accompaniment of his Violin Concerto, opus 61:

1 flute	2 horns
2 oboes	2 trumpets
2 clarinets	tympani
2 bassoons	strings

It is important to observe again that these instruments participated symphonically in a consummate fusion of the orchestra and solo violin.

CHAPTER TWO

LOUIS SPOHR

SPOHR[1] endeavored to make the violin concerto a substantial and superior composition, free from the artificial bravura practices of the time. His idols were Mozart and Rode. From Mozart, he took the standard concerto form and much of his transparency, clarity, and precision of detail. Concerning Rode, he expressed himself as follows: "The oftener I heard him, the more

---

1. Louis Spohr (1784-1859) was born in the German duchy of Braunschweig. After limited study of violin and theory, he succeeded to a position as violinist in the court orchestra of the Duke of Braunschweig. The Duke resolved to assume responsibility for the education of the young musician and secured Franz Eck as his pedagogue. Eck was about to embark from Hamburg (April 30, 1802) on a concert tour, and it became necessary for Spohr to accompany him. From Hamburg the two musicians journeyed to Russia, where they met Clementi, Field, and other notable persons. Spohr informs us (*Selbstbiographie,* Vol. I, p. 21) that he was very assiduous during this tour of fourteen months, for he practiced ten hours daily, in addition to composing, painting, and reading.

In 1804 he undertook his first concert tour as a virtuoso and composer, and met with extraordinary success. During the ensuing year he accepted a position as concertmaster in the orchestra of the Duke of Gotha. From 1812 to 1815 he held an important position in Vienna. It was during this time that he met Beethoven. In 1822 Spohr began his engagement as *Hofkapellmeister* in Kassel. He remained in that capacity for thirty-five years, during which period he composed approximately two hundred works of every genre.

Spohr was distinguished not only as a violinist and composer, but also as a conductor and pedagogue. His *Violinschule* (1831) became a milepost in violin pedagogy.

enraptured I became with his playing. Indeed, I had no scruples about placing Rode's style (which recalled his great master, Viotti) above that of my own teacher, Eck; and through assiduous practice, I endeavored to make it my own so far as possible."[2] This influence is especially manifest in the elegant and florid melodic style, the Alla polacca dance movements, and specific passage types.

While Spohr contributed materially to the preservation of many sterling Classical qualities (as may be observed in his first five violin concertos), he became far more significant for his efforts to achieve a new Romantic mode of expression. He accepted the programmatic, and exploited irregular formal structures, such as the recitative, thus affecting the later work of Maurer, David, Vieuxtemps, and Bruch. He employed folk tunes, syncopation, bold melodic leaps, various pedal-point effects, sudden interchanges of major and minor tonalities, direct modulations to mediant and sub-mediant keys (in some instances prior to Beethoven and Schubert), enharmony, and a profuse display of chromaticism.

Riemann insisted that Spohr's cultivation of a special chromatic style was due to his violinistic and sentimental predilections: "On the violin, chromaticism is at least half *portamento*. About the time of Spohr's appearance as a composer, the *portamento* was a familiar virtuosic effect of string players; and it is hardly necessary, therefore, to recall Spohr's inclination to the sentimental and trivial as an explanation of his use of this mannerism."[3] There is little doubt that Spohr's chromatic idioms influenced the works of Bohrer, David, Liszt, Wagner, and other Romanticists.

If ornamentation in art be a creation of the imagination, it is joined to inspiration and reflection in some of the copiously embellished slow movements of Spohr. Classical predecessors, for example, Tartini and Viotti, wrote only bare sketches of their Adagios; for they desired that the soloist have ample opportunity

2. L. Nohl, *Spohr* (Musiker-Biographien, Reclam, Vol. VII), p. 17.
3. H. Riemann, *Geschichte der Musik seit Beethoven*, pp. 193-194.

to exhibit his improvisatory skill. But this practice led to abuses, so that it became necessary for composers to write out precisely the embellishments they intended.[4]

Although Spohr's application of violin technique was marked by no striking innovations, it was, nevertheless, distinguished for its solidity and effectiveness. Spohr made no use of certain piquant bowings such as the *spiccato, sautillé,* and *saltando.* Neither did he use artificial harmonics; for he regarded them as grotesque and trivial, despite the fact that they constituted one of the scintillating features of Paganini's virtuosic style.[5]

Like Paganini, Rode, Kreutzer, Baillot, Lafont, and other early contemporaries, Spohr found it necessary to "humor" his public frequently with new works.[6] He wrote his first five violin concertos before Beethoven had completed his epochal Concerto, opus 61; and, by the year 1828, Spohr had already published eleven violin concertos. Was it not strange that neither he nor his contemporaries gave attention to the merits of the Beethoven Concerto?

ANALYSES

Concerto No. I in A major, Opus I [7]

The First Concerto, in A major, was composed during the tour with Franz Eck.[8] Despite its obvious deficiencies, the work was

4. "Because of the fact that followers invariably sought to outdo their predecessors, also desiring to add something new, there arose, ultimately, such arbitrary conceptions and lack of taste in embellishment that composers found it advisable to write out the necessary embellishments, at first in small notes, leaving their values to the discretion of the performer, and later in large notes with precise indications of their time values."—L. Spohr, *Violinschule*, p. 154.

5. "In spite of the recent sensation created by the famous Paganini with his . . . brilliant execution of the antiquated and already forgotten (artificial) harmonics, and despite the fact that such an example may be very enticing, I must nevertheless caution all young violinists not to lose time, and neglect more useful material in the study of them."—*Ibid.,* p. 108.

6. "In order to prepare myself for an ensuing concert tour, it became necessary for me to compose with great assiduity."—Spohr, *Selbstbiographie,* Vol. I, p. 72.

7. Leipzig: Breitkopf und Härtel, orchestra parts and pianoforte score.

8. See note I in this chapter.

considered a "respectable" achievement for a musician only eighteen years of age.

The opening movement (Allegro vivace) has a sonata form with
a double exposition (embracing an orchestral exposition of eighty-
seven measures). The second theme, in the dominant key, and
with symmetrical four-measure phrases,

recurs in the development section transposed to C major. Little
effort is made by the composer to manipulate and exploit thematic
material, thus divulging a weakness that may be regarded as persistent and typical.

The second movement is a Siciliano, in the lowered sub-mediant
key (F). This traditional old dance was attractive not only to
Spohr, but also to Bach, Händel, Kreutzer, and other composers.
The pastoral melody has a characteristic rhythm:

It is adroitly embellished:

In the concluding section, there is another freely ornamented
version of the melody:

The final movement is a rather weak Polonaise[9] with monotonous themes and elementary double stops. This dance type, like the Rondo russe, Bolero, and Tambourin, was brought to central Europe by Lolli, Giornovicchi, Viotti, Rode, Kreutzer, and other touring artists,[10] and it became a favorite "drawing-room" piece of the nineteenth century.

Concerto No. II in D minor, Opus 2[11]

The Second Concerto, dating from 1804, exhibits an unusual combination of free and conventional traits. The irregular form of the Allegro moderato is of special interest. A march theme

appears at the beginning of the orchestral exposition. Observe, also, its subsequent recurrence (meas. 151) in the raised sub-mediant key (B minor). In the solo exposition it is displaced by what may be a derivative presentation:

9. French: *polonaise;* Italian: *polacca;* Polish: *polonez.*
10. Schering, *Geschichte des Instrumentalkonzerts,* p. 170.
11. Peters edition, No. 1098 a, pianoforte score.

The harmonic structure of the movement is elemental and conservative.

The Adagio is lyrical. Mellifluous thirds and sixths and various trill effects point to the individualistic manner of the composer's violin playing:

As Spohr was a very expressive player on his instrument, it was quite natural that his compositions, especially the slow movements and recitatives, would reflect this quality.

The concluding Alla polacca is characterized by a "deutsche Behäbigkeit" together with French influences. The first theme displays a jerky dance rhythm:

Legato passages with incisive short trills are utilized with trenchant effect:

Concerto No. III in C major, Opus 7[12]

Concerto No. III was completed in Altenburg in 1805, and was dedicated to Rodolphe Kreutzer. Despite its weak rhythmic structure (almost invariably a cardinal defect in Spohr's compositions), the work merits greater attention than has been given it.

The first movement consists of an Adagio introduction of seven measures (C minor) followed by an Allegro (C major). A promi-

12. Leipzig: Peters, orchestra parts and pianoforte score.

nent figure,[13] taken from the first measure, recurs in the declamatory theme:

The Siciliano is rather similar to that employed in Concerto No. I. It also has a coherent ternary form. The first section is a brief orchestral introduction, which is reproduced with abbreviations and modifications in the concluding section. Engel speaks of the "liebeselig," Romantic qualities of this worthy movement.[14]

The concluding Rondo alla polacca reveals the dominant influence of Rode. We observe, moreover, Spohr's chromaticism, firm staccati, and various trill effects. Immediately preceding the final appearance of the main theme, there is a protracted cadence:

13. A figure is defined as a fragment of a motive.

14. H. Engel, *Das Instrumentalkonzert* (Führer durch den Konzertsaal, begonnen von H. Kretzschmar. *Die Orchestermusik*, Vol. III), p. 288.

One notes in the above example the persistent repetition of the tone *e* as a pedal against alternating tonic and dominant harmonies. Similar cadential effects were utilized by Mendelssohn,[15] Debussy, Stravinsky, and other composers. A contrasting section discloses these precipitous leaps:

Solo Violin (meas. 143)

Concerto No. IV, Opus 10,[16] and Concerto No. V, Opus 17[17]

The Fourth Concerto in B minor was composed in Braunschweig in 1804, thus actually preceding Concerto No. III. The Fifth Concerto in E-flat major was probably written in 1806.

The Allegro moderato movements of both concertos are lacking in individuality. The second movement (Adagio ma non troppo) of Concerto No. V is superior to the prosaic Adagio of the Fourth Concerto. A dramatic and florid "Klagegesang" in the middle section foreshadows the significant Adagio of Concerto, opus 47 ("in Form einer Gesangsszene").

A brief, concluding Rondo Allegretto in Concerto No. IV has some affinity with the work of Rode. The Rondo of Concerto No. V suffers from prolix thematic, harmonic, and rhythmic structures; but the cadenza is effective in its technical display.

Concerto No. VI in G minor, Opus 28[18]

The composer had a high regard for his Sixth Concerto. This work, composed in 1808, is of particular interest because of its exotic melodies, recitatives, and varied harmonic structures.

15. See *infra*, p. 70.
16. Berlin: Simrock, orchestra parts; Leipzig: Peters, pianoforte score.
17. Zürich: Naegeli, orchestra parts.
18. Peters edition, No. 1098 a, pianoforte score.

The main theme of the first movement has the bravura style of the "Directoiregeiger":

One of the numerous specimens of chromaticism in this movement is quoted. Note the oppositional rhythms and sequential structures:

The second movement (Recitativo andante—Allegro molto—Adagio—Recitativo andante) is a free and declamatory movement, which Spohr adapted to the violin concerto with admirable effect. The recitatives, antiphony between orchestra and solo, *Gesangsmanier,* embellishments, and chromaticism indicate a stylistic relationship with the first movement of the Concerto, opus 47 ("in Form einer Gesangsszene"). The Adagio section, in the key of B-flat, seems to predominate.

The finale, Alla Spagnola (Tempo di polacca), is marked by the composer's use of Spanish folk tunes. An example is cited with this motive from the first theme:

Spohr said about the Spanish tunes in this finale: "I heard them sung to the accompaniment of the guitar by a Spanish soldier who was billeted with me. I noted down whatever pleased me and wove it into my Rondo. In order to lend it a more genuine Spanish character, I also imitated in the orchestra score the guitar accompaniment precisely as I had heard it from the Spaniard."[19] The guitar accompaniment referred to has this rhythm:

This early adaptation of folk melodies to the violin concerto[20] would indicate that Spohr was a forerunner of composers such as Joachim, Brahms, Dvořák, Grieg, Lalo, Debussy, D'Indy, Ravel, and the various Russians—all of whom utilized nationalistic and folk expressions.

Concerto No. X in A minor, Opus 62[21]

The Tenth Concerto is a "Paradepferd" that dates from 1810-1811. It preceded Concertos Nos. VII, VIII, and IX, and was contemporaneous with the composer's First Symphony.

The irregular first movement (Adagio—Allegro) is not in the sonata form. There is a bare suggestion of the return of the main theme in the dominant major key (meas. 209); and a derivative theme is observed in the coda. The second theme appears but

19. Spohr, *Selbstbiographie*, Vol. I, p. 133.
20. The Concerto in G minor was published before 1828. See *infra*, p. 149.
21. Peters edition, orchestra parts and pianoforte score.

once in the movement (meas. 157). The following double-stops are exceedingly difficult when executed in rapid tempo:

(meas. 68)

The second movement (Adagio) is somewhat reminiscent of Mozart, while the concluding Rondo (Vivace) has much in common with the finale of the composer's Ninth Concerto.

Concerto No. VII in E minor, Opus 38[22]

Concerto No. VII, together with Concertos Nos. VIII and IX, has a place among the significant literature written for the violin during the Romantic era. It was composed in 1815, after Spohr had completed the opera *Faust* and a substantial quantity of chamber music.

The Allegro has an orchestral exposition (52 measures) with an important tonal motto:

(meas. 1)

The first theme is marked by bold leaps and anacrustic rhythms:

A new theme (C major) with suspensions, double-stops, and double trills is set forth in the development:

22. Peters edition, No. 1098 a; also Carl Fischer, No. 709.

The reprise commences (meas. 240) with a restatement of the
second theme in the parallel major key (E); and there is a suggestion of the first theme near the end of the movement.

The dramatic quality, unity and coherence, and "rhythmische
Feinheiten" of the Adagio are superior compositional traits. The
harmonies, also, are of special interest because of the idiomatic
enharmonic and chromatic progressions:

The e-flat (meas. 26) should be written as d-sharp, according to
the analysis. The dotted quarter notes in measure 25 constitute a
motive that is used repeatedly in the bass part.

A piquant melody, that again recalls Rode, constitutes the main
theme of the Rondo:

The formal design embraces the sections: A — B — A — C — B —
A — coda. Section C, in the lowered sub-mediant key (C major),
is broad and peremptory:

Concerto No. VIII in A minor, Opus 47
  (in Form einer Gesangsszene)[23]

This important composition was written in 1816 while the composer was touring in Switzerland. The première took place in La Scala, Milan, on September 27 of that year,[24] and was a notable success. "To some extent in this concerto, Spohr enunciated his violinistic creed; for he united dramatic, melodious, and technical *(violintechnischen)* elements, and infused them with the Romanticism of his lyrical nature."[25]

In the Allegro molto the composer disregards the sonata form and adapts a free recitative to the opening movement of the concerto. It will be recalled that the recitative had been employed in the second movement of Spohr's Sixth Concerto, and that analogous instrumental arias were found in the concertos of eighteenth-century masters. But it was Spohr's ". . . achievement to have adapted these forms (originally vocal) with conviction and taste, and also with more logicality than did his predecessors."[26] The solo violin and orchestra carry on an energetic dialogue in which the former provides a "klagende, fragende, leidenschaftliche Antwort" to the orchestra. The phrase quoted below manifests itself repeatedly in the orchestra:

The Adagio, despite its vacuous orchestral accompaniment, is a distinctive movement with fine emotional contrasts, rich embel-

23. Leipzig: Eulenberg, orchestra score; Peters and Schirmer editions, pianoforte scores.

24. This was a short time before Spohr met Paganini in Venice, an occasion which he described as follows: "He visited me early this morning; and so, finally, I made the personal acquaintance of this miracle man about whom I had heard almost every day since my sojourn in Italy."—*Selbstbiographie*, Vol. I, p. 300.

25. P. Schwers and M. Friedland, *Das Konzertbuch*, Vol. II (*Instrumental-Solokonzerte*), p. 51.   26. *Ibid.*, pp. 51-52.

lishments, and expressive violin idioms. Its form is ternary. At the beginning there is a poignant theme given to the first violins, complemented by the clarinet and flute:

This acquires a florid treatment when it is taken up by the solo violin (meas. 9). The second and contrasting section presents a bold and impassioned theme on the G string:

Note the audacious leaps in the solo part, and the ascent of the first violins high above the solo. The final section, an abbreviated and modified version of the first, leads into an Andante recitative that serves as the transition to the ensuing movement. The double-stop effects for the solo violin are particularly striking.

The harmonic scheme of the movement is conservative. The first section emphasizes the principal key (F). Section II begins in the flat mediant key (A-flat major), and alludes to the keys of F minor, E-flat major, B-flat minor, and C major before returning to F major for the restatement of the first section. The Andante transition proceeds from F major to D minor and A minor—the latter constituting the tonality of the concluding movement.

The Allegro moderato is on an equally high niveau with the other two movements of this concerto. It is a rondo: A (introductory presentation) — A — B — A — A — cadenza — coda. The main theme is imposing with its trill successions and heavy accents:

The cadenza, written out by Spohr, begins in measure 206. Harmonically, the movement is of considerable interest. An example of the numerous suspensions is quoted:

A smooth enharmonic modulation in the contrasting section

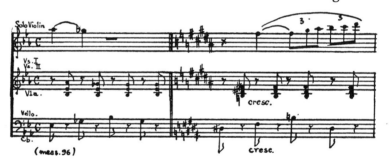

typifies the "romantische Seele" of the composer.

Concerto No. IX in D minor, Opus 55[27]

The crowning achievement of Spohr's violin compositions is his Ninth Concerto. This work dates from the year 1820, and

27. André and Litolff editions, pianoforte scores.

followed very soon after the composer's Second Symphony. The elegance of the expression, the opulent modulatory harmonies, thematic manipulations, and the virtuosic quality of the solo violin part merit praise.

In the Allegro, after an orchestral exposition of fifty-four measures in which there is frequent reference to motive X, the solo violin enters with a long chromatic scale that leads into the pensive first theme:

An eloquent melody, ascending to the upper registers, constitutes the second theme:

This is reproduced an octave lower, and then succeeded by coloristic chromatic modulations (meas. 113-117). Other modulations are conspicuous, for example:

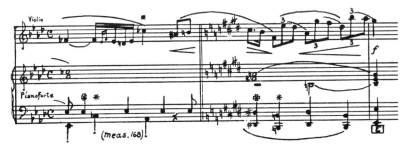

The tones e-flat[28] and c-flat are employed as enharmonic pivots from which the d-sharp and b are derived. There are numerous

28. These are written as quarter notes without syncopation in the Litolff edition.

other striking traits in this Allegro, for example, these extraordinary leaps in the solo exposition:

and the use of the "Viotti" bowing:[29]

The Rococo elegance of the Adagio is reminiscent of Mozart. After a brief introduction in the orchestra, there is an aristocratic melody with ornate lines given to the solo violin:

The key is F major, and the formal design is binary, with these sections: A — B — A — B — coda. The latter part (meas. 90) contains embellishments such as this descending chromatic scale:

The accompaniment in the movement is unimpressive.

The Rondo allegretto, which Engel, however, termed "konventionell und matt,"[30] has imposing virtuosic qualities and Romantic emotional contrasts. The design of the movement embraces these

29. Baillot, in *L'Art du Violon*, terms this bowing "la saccade." Spohr, however, uses the designation "Viotti-Bogenstrich" in his *Violinschule*.

30. Engel, *Das Instrumentalkonzert* (Führer durch den Konzertsaal, begonnen von H. Kretzschmar. *Die Orchestermusik*, Vol. III), p. 291.

divisions: A — B — C — A — B — C — A — coda. The main
theme is spirited and jovial:

Figure *z* is utilized in a contrapuntal manner (meas. 61-75)—a
rather infrequent procedure of Spohr:

Section B makes its entrance with incisive staccatos and trill effects:

This section concludes (meas. 127) in the key of C-sharp. Then
with the tone *c*-sharp as a pivot, the key of A major is chosen for
an episode that may be designated as the beginning of section C:

There are trenchant passages with heavy accentuations on the
off-beat:

The Last Concertos

Of the remaining violin concertos, No. XI was published before 1828; Nos. XII, XIII, and XIV were published between 1828 and 1844; and Concerto No. XV appeared in print between 1844 and 1851.[31] Special attributes of these varied works include: formal experiments (Concertos Nos. XII and XIV); chromatic idioms (first movement of Concerto No. XI, and third movement of Concerto No. XV); and frequent metrical changes in the Larghetto of Concerto No. XII. Of some interest, also, is the observation that the movements of Concerto No. XV, opus 128,[32] are linked together by means of harmonic transitions.

The substantial first movement of Concerto No. XI in G major, opus 70,[33] begins with an Adagio introduction of twenty-two measures. This is followed by an Allegro vivace, in which the principal theme is immediately announced by the orchestra. Subsequently, the violin takes up this theme in a virile rhythm:

Note the irregular length of the phrase and the chromatics of the

31. See *infra*, p. 149.   32. Hamburg and Leipzig: Schuberth.
33. Schirmer and Peters editions, pianoforte scores.

accompaniment. Substantial thematic allusions are made in the development and coda, but the theme does not appear in the reprise.

The first movement of Concerto No. XII in A major, opus 79,[34] has a free and unconventional design. The movement is labeled Andante grave, and comprises an orchestral introduction (17 measures) and a solo recitative (36 measures). The florid and dramatic character of the latter section is reminiscent of similar expressions in the composer's Sixth and Eighth Concertos.

The opening movement of Concerto No. XV in E minor, opus 128,[35] sets forth a new theme (meas. 114) in the development section. Near the close there is some emphasis on the dominant and tonic keys, after which a simple transition (8 measures) leads directly into the succeeding Larghetto.

The Adagio of Concerto No. XI has a plaintive theme

which is remarkably similar to a theme in the Andante of Mayseder's Concerto, opus 22.[36] The effect of a pedal-point against pompous arpeggios in the solo violin part (meas. 51) is striking:

34. Peters and Universal editions, pianoforte scores. The Concerto was also published as Concertino No. I.

35. Hamburg and Leipzig: Schuberth and Co., orchestra parts and pianoforte score.   36. See *infra*, p. 44.

We might also refer to a passage from Concerto No. XIII, opus 92,[37] in which Spohr exhibits his favorite pedal effects:

More significant, however, are the change from major to minor and the syncopated effects obtained with the ties in the notation of the solo part.

The coherence of the Larghetto movement of Concerto No. XII is meritorious. An orchestral introduction of four measures precedes an ornate theme in the solo violin part. In this theme we discover a motto (meas. 12) that is of vital importance in the movement:

This is subsequently given varied positions in the measure:

Another feature of this movement is the recurring metrical changes. Thus we observe:

12-8, meas. 1	9-8, meas. 30
9-8, meas. 5	6-8, meas. 42
6-8, meas. 24	9-8, meas. 48

3-8, meas. 50

37. Mainz: Schott, pianoforte score. Published by Breitkopf und Härtel as Concertino No. II.

The last change serves as the metrical basis for the transition into the Alla polacca.

The rondo of Concerto No. XI has a monotonous rhythmic structure. (It will be recalled that Spohr's rhythms are generally weak and lacking in diversity.) The reversion to the antiquated Alla polacca type of finale in the Twelfth Concerto harks back to Spohr's early work. He last employed it in Concerto No. VI, in which it was given a Spanish flavor.

Spohr was interested in that which was new; consequently as program music developed with the achievements of Beethoven, Berlioz, and Liszt, we find Spohr reverting to analogous programmatic correlations. Thus his symphonies, *Die Weihe der Töne* (1834), *Irdisches und Göttliches im Menschenleben* (1842), and *Die vier Jahreszeiten* (1850), followed this strong impulse to take music from its exclusive domain in order to associate it with poetry, drama, and other subjective expressions.

In Concerto No. XIV, opus 110,[38] the programmatic appellation, *Sonst und Jetzt,* was motivated by the adaptation of two familiar dance forms, the minuet *(Sonst),* and a more modern type *(Jetzt)*—the latter somewhat like a tarantella. The form is irregular. The graceful Tempo di menuett antico *(Sonst)* is a movement of considerable dimensions. It is interrupted by a bold and merry Vivace *(Jetzt)* in 2-4 meter. Subsequently, the minuet reasserts itself for a short time, after which the Vivace emerges again and continues to the close.

ORCHESTRATION

In the orchestration of the violin concertos Spohr remained behind the significant advances already effected in the expansion and development of the orchestral unit. The influence of contemporaries such as Beethoven, Weber, Marschner, and Berlioz had touched him but lightly. It is true, however, that he augmented the orchestra, but he did not exploit its possibilities for color and

38. Published by Schott as Concertino No. III.

real thematic participation. The solo violin dominated, autocratically, and the other parts remained subservient.[39] The violoncello and contrabass parts were almost invariably doubled, in accordance with the conservative traditions of Mozart and Haydn. A single orchestral instrument, the flute, was particularly favored, in that it was occasionally granted important solo entrances with thematic material and varied passages.

In Concertos Nos. III, V, VII, and IX Spohr used the antiquated clarino, a high solo trumpet with a narrow, flat mouthpiece.[40] In Concerto No. I the supporting orchestra was small:

2 flutes	2 horns
2 bassoons	strings

The accompaniment, even in the strings, was stereotyped. In Concerto No. II, 2 clarinets, 1 trombone, and 2 tympani were added. In Concerto No. III there were:

2 flutes	2 bassoons
2 oboes	2 horns
2 clarinets	2 clarini
strings	

In No. V the composer employed:

1 flute	3 horns
2 oboes	2 clarini
2 clarinets	tympani
2 bassoons	strings

39. Spohr informs us (*Selbstbiographie,* Vol. I, p. 11) that while he was in the employ of the Duke of Braunschweig the orchestra was scheduled to play a weekly concert. Not infrequently, however, a card game was in progress, and it became necessary to perform the entire program pianissimo, even omitting the trumpets and tympani from the instrumentation so as not to disturb the card players.

40. ". . . not ordinarily used as the name of an instrument, but rather as a designation for high trumpet parts in the seventeenth and eighteenth centuries. The execution of these parts required exceptional skill, being facilitated by the use of a narrow, flat, and broad-rimmed mouthpiece."—C. Sachs, *Real-Lexikon der Musikinstrumente,* p. 85.

In Concerto No. VII there were:

2 flutes	2 horns
2 oboes	2 trumpets
2 clarinets	tympani
2 bassoons	strings

Ultimately, in Concerto No. IX, progress is made with the following instrumentation:

2 flutes	2 horns
2 oboes	2 clarini
2 clarinets	3 trombones
2 bassoons	tympani
strings	

In Concerto No. XV there were pairs of wood-winds and trumpets, in addition to 4 horns, tympani, and strings. The accompaniment of this work is rather free and independent. The slow movements of all of the concertos were almost entirely accompanied by strings.

SUMMARY

There were both conservative and radical elements in Spohr's dual nature. The latter was reflected in the numerous innovations which we recount in these violin concertos. Movements were occasionally linked together, as in Concertos Nos. XII and XV. A serious and contemplative Adagio type was of special interest in Concertos Nos. II, VIII, IX, and XI. There was a departure from the conventional forms to the free recitative expressions in Concertos No. VI (second movement), No. VIII (first movement), and No. XII (first movement). In the latter two movements, and also in the first movement of Concerto No. X, the sonata form was entirely disregarded. Occasionally the first movements of concertos began with a slow introduction, as in Nos. III, X, and XI; and sometimes new themes were employed in the development or coda (Concertos No. XV and No. X). In Concerto No. VIII Spohr wrote out his violin cadenza and placed it in the finale; while on other occasions, he omitted it entirely (Concertos Nos. II, IX, XII).

Barring several exceptions, the foreign dance rhythms and folk tunes, which were evident in the early works, received little attention in the later ones. Thus we find no Sicilianos after Concerto No. III; and the Alla polacca is also discarded in the later works, excepting Concertos Nos. XII and XIII. The insertion of Spanish folk tunes in Concerto No. VI was of exceptional interest.

Spohr's rejection of certain piquant bowings and artificial harmonics was peculiar to his style of violin playing. Here, however, he was not farsighted. His weaknesses as a creator were of such a nature that we can hardly classify him among the greatest composers. He lacked ". . . Bach's austere grandeur, Händel's freedom, and Beethoven's flights of the imagination."[41] There is also some justification for Riemann's opinion: "The secret of Beethoven's rhythmic and thematic conceptions *(Themengestaltung),* and the spirit of modern polyphony with the participation of all voices were never revealed to him. . . ."[42]

He gave us, nevertheless, some elegant, lyrical expressions and Romantic harmonic idioms, with the emphasis on mediant and sub-mediant key relationships, enharmony, and chromaticism. He had a predilection for a melodious, homophonic style; and his formal experiments were among the important contributions of the time. With his fifteen violin concertos, Spohr won for himself a conspicuous place in the history of nineteenth-century musical literature.

He lived in an age when Beethoven, Cherubini, Rossini, Schubert, Weber, Marschner, Paganini, Berlioz, Meyerbeer, Mendelssohn, Chopin, Schumann, and Liszt were performing

41. H. M. Schletterer, *Louis Spohr,* p. 133.
42. Riemann, *Geschichte der Musik seit Beethoven,* p. 201.

and composing their epochal music; when Hegel, Schleiermacher, Schopenhauer, Goethe, Novalis, Tieck, Jean Paul, Scott, Wordsworth, Coleridge, Byron, Shelley, Keats, and Carlyle were creating new worlds of philosophy and literature. He lived in an era when the momentous political exigencies caused by Napoleon, Metternich, and the revolutions of 1830 and 1848 were remaking the physiognomy of Europe; when science, through its multitudinous inventions, was revolutionizing western civilization.

THE VIRTUOSO CONCERTO

Among the composers of the violin concerto contemporary with Louis Spohr were a number of virtuosi who became more significant as performers than as creators. "Large numbers of these ... clever so-called priests of art toured the various countries. Everywhere they met with a hearty reception, if only because they knew how to tickle the ears of their auditors, impressing by technical dexterity and superficial brilliance; . . . or perhaps because they could hold the interest of the crowd by means of their outer appearance, their eccentric bearing, and the nebulous atmosphere created by the persistence of racy anecdotes about their personalities. . . ."[1]

Pre-eminent among these virtuosi was Nicolo Paganini. Although he was not German, he comes within the scope of this work because of the fact that he exerted such a vital influence on many of the German Romanticists. His extraordinary accomplishments as a performer, his bravura compositions, and his almost demoniacal personality ". . . went over the earth like a fructifying spring storm, inflaming kindred spirits, and opening up new paths in music."[2]

Also contemporary with Spohr were Anton Bohrer, Joseph Böhm, Joseph Mayseder, Ludwig W. Maurer, Karl J. Lipinski,

1. A. Niggli, "Nicolo Paganini," in *Sammlung musikalischer Vorträge,* hsg. von Paul Graf Waldersee, Vol. IV, p. 312.   2. *Ibid.,* p. 350.

Johann W. Kalliwoda, Wilhelm B. Molique, Heinrich W. Ernst, and Ferdinand David. Like Paganini, these composers were bizarre, sentimental, and eclectic. But they were good melodists; and their treatment of violin technique offers to the scholar an index of the concentration on this phase of virtuosic art during the first half of the nineteenth century. Bohrer, Böhm, Mayseder, and Maurer were particularly subject to the influence of the French exponents, Viotti, Rode, and Kreutzer. This is easily comprehensible if we remember that the latter artists toured much of Europe during the first part of the century and disseminated assiduously their gospel of violinistic art. Paganini did not play outside of Italy until 1828, and most of his works were published posthumously; consequently we shall mark his influence chiefly on the later Romanticists, such as Lipinski, Ernst, and others.

It is interesting to observe that these virtuosi had comparatively little schooling in musical composition. Nevertheless, they became exceptionally prolific and versatile, essaying not only the favorite polonaises, variations, marches, études, and potpourris, but also the large forms, such as symphonies and operas.

Nicolo Paganini

Paganini was born in Genoa on February 18, 1784. He studied the violin under the tutelage of his father before he was taken to local violinists of prominence. Through his own genius and the indomitable will of his father, he soon mastered the most complex technical problems. Two patrons provided further opportunity for his education by sending him to A. Rolla, a violinist in Parma. He was also given some instruction in composition by G. Ghiretti.

When Paganini was thirteen years old, he made his first concert tour, visiting Milan, Bologna, and other Italian cities. From 1801 to 1804 he withdrew from his public career. During these years he studied the guitar[3] and also very probably acquainted himself with

3. Paganini published twelve Sonatas for Violin and Guitar, opera 2 and 3; and six Quartets for Violin, Viola, Guitar, and Violoncello, opera 4 and 5.

Locatelli's *L'Arte di Nuova Modulazione*. This latter work, according to Fétis, opened up a new world of ideas to Paganini. After associating himself (1805-1808) with the private musical establishment of Napoleon's sister, the Princess of Lucca and Piombo, Paganini resumed his concert journeys. In 1828 he gave twenty concerts in Vienna before undertaking a tour of Germany, England, France, and other European countries. Wherever he played, he captivated both musicians and public.[4]

The significant characteristics of Paganini's art are violinistic and technical: the cultivation and development of G-string playing; an unprecedented facility in double-stops and chord playing; ascending and descending glissandi; facile use of single and double harmonics; dexterous left-hand pizzicati, occasionally involving the combination of a pizzicato accompaniment with its own melody; extension of the playing range to the highest registers of the violin; the use of the *scordatura;* and a command of bowing technique that enabled the performance of extraordinary staccati and other exceptional effects. The persistently simple harmonic structures and vacuous accompaniments in Paganini's compositions were, however, serious defects.

From his two available violin concertos,[5] published posthumously,[6] only the first movement of the Concerto in E-flat (D),

4. Shops were bedecked with his portrait; and there were Paganini hats, bows, cigar boxes, pipes, lamps, etc. Some of these articles were adorned with figures of a violin and bells because of the popularity of the composer's *Rondo à la Clochette.*—Niggli, "Nicolo Paganini," in *Sammlung musikalischer Vorträge,* hsg. von Paul Graf Waldersee, Vol. IV, p. 315.

5. In addition to these and other violin concertos, Paganini wrote: *Twenty-four Caprices,* opus 1 (published during the composer's lifetime); *Le Streghe; Il Moto Perpetuo; I Palpiti; Non più Mesta; Variations on "God Save the King";* and other works.

6. "Paganini knew that interest in his concerts would diminish if he published the compositions that he played. He resolved, therefore, not to have these works printed until after he had concluded his tours and had retired from the career of a performing artist. On his travels he carried with him only the orchestra parts of the compositions which he regularly played; and no one ever saw the solo parts of these works. . . ."—Fétis, *Biographie Universelle des Musiciens,* Vol. VI, p. 417.

opus 6, and the third movement *(Rondo à la Clochette)* of the Concerto in B minor, opus 7, are now performed in public.

The Concerto in E-flat (D), opus 6,[7] was probably written during the second decade of the nineteenth century. It is as characteristically Italian as the operas of Rossini, Donizetti, and Bellini; and it betrays, too, the highly subjective temperament of the composer. The Allegro maestoso has an orchestral exposition of ninety-four measures, in which a poignant theme is enunciated in the dominant key:

A bravura first theme does not appear until the beginning of the solo exposition (meas. 95). The altered tuning of the solo violin,[8]

causing that part to be written in D major, enables the performer to make propitious use of the open strings. The solo exposition includes some brilliant passages in thirds, which were emulated by Lipinski and other writers:

The development brings forth "heroic" recitative passages:

7. Mayence: Chez les Fils de B. Schott, pianoforte score.

8. Despite the raised pitches, this tuning hardly constitutes an application of the *scordatura* because of the fact that the interval relationships are uniformly preserved. The following tunings, according to Baillot (*L'Art du Violon,* pp. 259-260), are representative examples of the *scordatura:*

An example of the *saltando*[9] is cited:

This bowing is also utilized in the piquant theme of the finale:

Other representative passages are displayed in this pyrotechnical rondo. There are, for example, difficult stretches for the left hand:

and a striking use of the high registers:

The original score of the work ostensibly required:[10]

2 flutes	2 trumpets
2 oboes	3 trombones
2 clarinets	tympani
1 bassoon	bass drum
1 contra-bassoon	cymbals
2 horns	strings

9. The slur is not indicated in this edition of the concerto; nevertheless, the passage is generally played with the *saltando* bowing as designated.

10. See F. B. Emery, *The Violin Concerto*, p. 138.

This would indicate an augmentation of the orchestral setting.

The first movement of the Concerto in B minor, opus 7,[11] reveals a galaxy of pyrotechnics such as chromatic octaves, broken thirds, double harmonics, and even harmonic trills:

The closing movement of this concerto is the celebrated *Rondo à la Clochette* (Allegro moderato) with which Paganini enthralled his audiences. It is in the form: A — B — A — C — A — coda. The main theme is illustrative of Paganini's humor:

Bell effects are made with harmonics:

Theme II (B major) provides a strong contrast:

We find a specimen of the "Viotti" bowing:[12]

11. Paris: H. Lemoine et Cie. Also, Mayence: Chez les Fils de B. Schott, piano-forte score.

12. See *supra,* Chap. II, note 29. This bowing style is not indicated in the Schott edition of the work, and may, therefore, be the insertion of an editor.

The following chromatic sixths are awkward:

Paganini's *blitzende* left-hand pizzicati are conspicuous in the movement:

The Adagios of both concertos are mediocre and uninteresting. They possess few of those characteristics indicated as having exerted such a conspicuous influence on the contemporary and subsequent writers of Romantic music.

Paganini's art affected directly the creativity of Mayseder, Maurer, Lipinski, Kalliwoda, Molique, Guhr,[13] Vieuxtemps, Wieniawski, Sarasate, and others. His magnetic influence also permeated in other directions. At his "instigation" Berlioz wrote the *Harold* Symphony, while Strauss and Lanner composed waltzes after him. Liszt transcribed the *Rondo à la Clochette* for the pianoforte; and both he and Schumann arranged some of the *Twenty-four Caprices* for the same instrument. "One may rightfully assert that the great revolutionary movement in piano playing and piano literature, which began in the thirties and at the head of which stood the . . . masters, Chopin, Schumann, and Liszt was hastened and profoundly influenced by the appearance

13. K. W. F. Guhr (1787-1848) entitled his First Concerto, opus 15, *Le Souvenir de Paganini*.

of Paganini. This was, perhaps, his outstanding mission in the history of art. . . ."[14]

The influence of Kreutzer is clearly discernible in Bohrer's violin concertos. The cantabile style, legato passages requiring exceptional bow control, and cadenza types are attestations of this influence.

The Allegro assai of Concerto No. IV, opus 27,[16] has a dance character. This may be inferred from the following theme in triple meter:

Cadenzas which are reminiscent of passages in Kreutzer's Twenty-Third Étude[17] are found in the Andante con moto quasi allegretto of the Fourth Concerto:

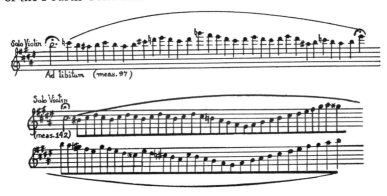

Note the extraordinarily long bowing stroke required, and the employment of French notation with long equal note values.

14. Niggli, "Nicolo Paganini," in *Sammlung musikalischer Vorträge*, hsg. von Paul Graf Waldersee, Vol. IV, pp. 349-350.

15. A. Bohrer (1783-1852) was descended from a musical family in Mannheim. He received his advanced training from Kreutzer and Rode. With his brother, Max, he made extensive concert tours throughout Europe.

16. Paris: Schlesinger, orchestra parts.   17. Peters edition.

In the Andante of Concerto No. V, opus 40,[18] there are similar passages. More interesting, however, is a protracted trill series:

A distinctive feature of the Adagio of Concerto No. I, opus 9,[19] is the use of the variation form. The Rondos of Concertos Nos. IV and V have virtuosic traits. In the second section of the former there are forty-one consecutive measures designated for the G string alone.

The score of Concerto No. V requires:

1 flute	2 horns
2 oboes	2 trumpets
2 clarinets	tympani
2 bassoons	strings

This is a Classical orchestra. The accompaniment is antiquated. In the first movement we discover a horn trill (Horn I, in D, meas. 47-50) on the note *d*, ornamenting a statement of the principal theme in the solo violin part. A rather extensive use of the *divisi* is made in the violin part of the Andante.

Joseph Böhm[20]

Böhm also merits attention because his work involves a fusion of German and French stylistic attributes. Concerto No. I in D major[21] discloses the influence of the composer's teacher, Rode. The exposition of the opening movement divulges a contrasting second theme (meas. 88-95) with angular leaps. In the course of

18. Mainz: Schott, orchestra parts.   19. Offenbach: André, orchestra parts.
20. Böhm (1793-1876) was a pupil of Rode. He became a leading exponent of the Viennese school of violin playing. From 1819 to 1848 he was a professor at the Vienna *Konservatorium*, where he taught such pupils as Ernst, G. Hellmesberger, and Joachim.   21. Paris: Schlesinger, orchestra parts.

the movement the composer evinces a predilection for light and delicate staccato bowings such as the *sautillé*[22] and *ricochet.*[23]

The scoring of Böhm's Concerto in D major requires the following instrumentation:

1 flute	2 horns
2 oboes	2 trumpets
2 clarinets	tympani
2 bassoons	strings

The orchestral accompaniment is effete and stereotyped.

JOSEPH MAYSEDER[24]

It has been said that Mayseder was much admired by Spohr and Joachim, and that he virtually dominated the musical life of Vienna from 1800 to 1830.[25] During his visit in Paris, in 1820, Mayseder associated with masters of the French school, such as Viotti, Cherubini, Kreutzer, Lafont, and Habaneck. This may have been partially responsible for the predominance of French traits in his violin compositions. He has an affinity with Viotti and Rode; but there is also the influence of Paganini. It may be asserted, moreover, that his work is anticipative of Ernst.[26]

22. See note 37 in this chapter.

23. The *ricochet* bowing stroke depends upon the elasticity of the bow. The impulse is given by the accentuation of the first tone of each group:

Fine examples of this bowing style may be found in Paganini, Caprice No. I of the *Twenty-four Caprices,* and also in the cadenza of the Mendelssohn Violin Concerto, opus 64.

24. Mayseder (1789-1863) was the son of an artist. He resided in Vienna and eventually became *Kammervirtuose* and *Direktor der kaiserlichen Hofkapellmusik* to Ferdinand I.

25. E. Hanslick, *Geschichte des Concertwesens in Wien,* Vol. II, p. 230.

26. Compare, for example, Mayseder's *Grosses Concertstück,* opus 47, with the Concerto in F-sharp minor, opus 23, by Ernst. A review of the latter is given *infra,* pp. 55-57.

Being essentially a virtuoso, Mayseder stressed violinistic par-
ticularities, such as double-stops, sonorous G-string passages, and
a variety of bowing styles. It is strange that he seldom employed
the firm staccato in his violin concertos, since he possessed an
exceptionally fine staccato. Other virtuosi, for example, Spohr,
Paganini, Kalliwoda, De Bériot, and Vieuxtemps, who commanded this effect, used it frequently in their works. On the other
hand, an artist such as Lipinski, who did not have a facile staccato,
would naturally avoid writing it.

Mayseder's Concerto No. I in A minor, opus 22,[27] has a march
theme in the first movement:

Motive H shows a striking resemblance to the beginning of the
Marcia funebre in Beethoven's Third Symphony. A lyrical second
theme (meas. 74) returns in the reprise; but the first theme does
not recur in that section.

A theme from the Adagio of Spohr's Eleventh Concerto[28] is
recalled in the exquisitely ornamented Andante:

The Rondo has a symmetrical first theme that is reminiscent of
Rode:

27. Vienna: Steiner, orchestra parts.   28. See *supra*, p. 27.

Some of the passage types also reflect the French influence; but others are quite independent:

Concerto No. III in D major, opus 28,[29] is less attractive than the one previously reviewed. The Adagio, in the parallel minor key (D), has a conventional ternary form. Immediately before the close of the movement there is a fermata with an indication that the soloist may interpose his own cadenza. This procedure in the slow movement was orthodox with the Classicists, but rather exceptional for the Romantic composers. The Rondo contains a fine example of the composer's transparent melos:

The instrumentation of both concertos is conservative. Concerto No. I includes:

2 flutes	2 trumpets
2 clarinets	bass trombone
2 bassoons	tympani
2 horns	strings

Concerto No. III is scored for pairs of wood-winds (including oboes), horns, clarini, tympani, and strings. The accompaniment is entirely subservient.

29. Berlin: Schlesinger, orchestra parts.

Ludwig Wilhelm Maurer[30]

Maurer stands out from his contemporaries, excepting Spohr and Paganini, because of his meritorious efforts to create violin music that was not prescriptive. He experimented with forms and introduced Russian folk tunes into one of his concertos, thus foreshadowing the nationalistic trend that was destined to become a vital musical force during the century.

Despite these endeavors, his work bears the stamp of French masters, Viotti, Rode, and Baillot. Maurer became acquainted with Rode and Baillot in Riga in 1806, and he is reputed to have had some instruction from Rode. The French influence is perceived in (1) the Alla polacca rondos with minore and majore sections, (2) the graceful and lyrical character of the themes, (3) the cadenzas and diverse passage types, and (4) the variety of bowing styles, notably the employment of the *sautillé*.[31]

Specific traits of Concertos Nos. I, II, V, VI, and VII will be reviewed.

The sonata form is used in the first movement of Concerto No. VI in E minor;[32] but in the reprise, the restatement of the second theme precedes that of the first theme. Some of the violin idioms are quite original:

In the second movement of Concerto No. I in G minor,[33] a florid recitative (Allegro assai) of forty measures leads into an Adagio

30. Maurer was born in Potsdam in 1789. In 1806 he undertook a concert tour of Russia, an event that was destined to be of great importance in his subsequent career. In 1817 he achieved a notable success as a virtuoso in Berlin, Paris, and other musical centers. The years 1819-1832 were spent in Hannover, after which Maurer went again to Russia. He died in St. Petersburg in 1878. The *Symphonie Concertante* for Four Violins and Orchestra was better known than the composer's other works.   31. See note 37 in this chapter.

32. Leipzig: Peters, orchestra parts.   33. Leipzig: Peters, orchestra parts.

cantabile. This recitative recalls Spohr. A large part of the Adagio affettuoso in Concerto No. V[34] is given over to a cadenza. A florid melody

is adroitly modified when it recurs in part 3:

The theme of the Adagio in Concerto No. VII[35] consists of two phrases of irregular length (8 and 14 measures), a rather unusual departure from the conventional four-measure phrase plan.

The concluding movements of these concertos seem more interesting than the preceding movements. The adaptation of folk tunes and formal innovations is especially significant. In Concerto No. V a scherzo is employed as the finale. This is a departure from the customary rondo types.[36] The movement commences with an introductory Lento (5 measures), in which there is a modulation from F major (the tonality of the preceding movement) to A major. Theme I is a period of eight measures, the first phrase of which is quoted:

34. Leipzig: Peters, orchestra parts.   35. Leipzig: Peters, orchestra parts.
36. Vieuxtemps, subsequently, utilized a scherzo in his Fourth Concerto, opus 31; however, it was not the closing movement.

The *sautillé*,[37] a *leggiero* bowing exploited by Böhm, Paganini, Mendelssohn, Joachim, and others, is utilized here with scintillating effect.

It is in the Rondo moderato of Concerto No. VI that Maurer introduces the Russian folk tunes. The first theme is a melancholy *Air russe,* in the Aeolian mode:

Observe the five-measure phrases and the predominance of motive repetitions. The element of repetition is an important psychological characteristic of folk music and poetry.[38] The second theme is a lively *Air baschkir* in a pentatonic mode, ornamented with grace-note flourishes:

Here the repetition is even more striking; and the effect is equally felicitous. The adaptation of these folk melodies was a result of Maurer's long residence in Russia. In their use, the composer, like Spohr, presaged the significant emphasis on nationalistic expressions that evolved with the work of Joachim, Liszt, Brahms,

---

37. "...the *sautillé* is produced by allowing the middle part of the bow to rebound lightly on the string...This bouncing effect is induced by relaxing the fingers on the bow, and by applying the *detaché* stroke to a minute part of the bow. By this means, one can achieve nuances of exceptional lightness. The *sautillé* differs from the more ample bow stroke of the *detaché,* and it differs from the *spiccato* in that the bow remains on the string." Adapted from M. Brenet, *Dictionnaire Pratique de la Musique,* p. 400.

38. In poetry the devices of alliteration, assonance, and the refrain are manifestations of this principle.

Dvořák, Debussy, Grieg, and the various Russian Romanticists.
The influence of Rode seems evident in the rondo of Concerto
No. II:[39]

It recalls a dance theme from Rode's Seventh Concerto:

The instrumentation of Maurer's Concerto No. I embraces:

1 flute	2 horns
2 oboes	2 clarini
2 clarinets	tympani
2 bassoons	strings

In Concerto No. V the clarinets and clarini are omitted, but a
bass trombone is added. In No. VI, 2 flutes and 3 horns represent
the augmentations. With Maurer, as with Spohr and the other
virtuosi of this period, the solo violin dominates autocratically over
an accompaniment that is devoid of individuality.

KARL JOSEPH LIPINSKI[40]

Although his musicianship was profoundly respected by his
contemporaries,[41] Lipinski's four violin concertos appear to be of
relatively little musical value. The brilliance and *bizarrerie* of
his virtuosic style reflect a zealous admiration for Paganini.

39. Leipzig: Peters, orchestra parts.
40. Lipinski (1790-1861) was born in Poland. During his early years as a
student he studied both violoncello and violin. After extensive tours he settled in
Dresden (1839), and remained there until the last year of his life. As a virtuoso
Lipinski ranked with Paganini, Spohr, and Ernst.
41. It will be recalled that Schumann dedicated the *Carnaval*, opus 9, to Lipinski.

The Concerto *Militaire* (No. II, in D major, opus 21)[42] was for a long time a veritable *tour de force* among violinists. Like the prevalent "Schlachtenkonzerte mit Kanonendonner," this work was the product of an era fraught with political changes and upheavals. The strong and heroic emotions were dominant qualities of this style.

The Allegro marziale of this concerto is somewhat irregular in form. After a protracted orchestral exposition (122 measures),[43] there are introductory phrases in a virile march rhythm:

The principal theme begins in measure 154. In the reprise (meas. 345) there is a recurrence of the main theme; but the second theme is omitted. Like most of the composers of the virtuoso concerto, Lipinski confines the development section almost entirely to the display and manipulation of violin passages. He gives

42. Leipzig: Peters, orchestra parts; Breitkopf und Härtel, pianoforte score. Engel says that the Fourth Concerto in G major ". . . ist das der Nachwelt noch bekannte Militärkonzert."—*Das Instrumentalkonzert,* p. 286. Emery, however, agrees with the author that the Second Concerto is the *Militaire.*

43. This long tutti was abbreviated to 31 measures in a comparatively recent edition by H. Sitt, published by Eulenberg.

little attention to the necessity for real thematic manipulation. The violin idioms include these chromatic thirds and octaves:

The Adagio più tosto andante is in the sub-mediant key (B minor). A section labeled "un poco animato" (meas. 69) recalls to us the Adagio religioso of Vieuxtemps' Fourth Concerto, opus 31.

In the Rondo (Allegretto) there are *sautillé* passages which, if played *sul ponticello*,[44] as this edition indicates, would be considered a rarity in violin technique:

The author has seen another edition in which this bowing style was not designated; and it is therefore probable that the composer did not desire the rather impracticable *sul ponticello* effect. Incidentally, there is not a single example of the firm staccato in this concerto. Lipinski did not possess a staccato, and would not, therefore, be inclined to utilize that effect in his compositions.

The accompaniment of the Concerto *Militaire* comprises:

1 piccolo	4 horns
1 flute	2 clarini
2 oboes	4 trombones
2 clarinets	tympani
2 bassoons	strings

44. *Sul ponticello* is executed with the bow very close to the bridge and with the bow hair turned outward. The principal difficulty consists in maintaining the same position so that the sound will be a "heftig vibrierender Ton" with a metallic and raucous quality.

The augmentation of the brass choir represents some advance in the dimensions of the orchestral setting for works of this genre.

Johann Wenzeslaus Kalliwoda[45]

Despite the fact that Kalliwoda's compositions appear to be somewhat lacking in originality, they were highly esteemed during the composer's lifetime. Schumann, for example, commented on Kalliwoda's Fifth Symphony as follows: "... It is quite unusual and unique in the symphony world; for it has tenderness and charm from beginning to end." And further on, "Thus we greet in Kalliwoda a perennially green tree in the forest of German musician-poets. ..."[46] Kalliwoda's violin compositions embody a fusion of German and French traits. This is apparent in the forms, thematic structures, and technical idioms. We observe, moreover, an affinity with Paganini and Sarasate.[47]

The Allegro maestoso of the Concerto in E major, opus 9,[48] features a bravura theme with audacious leaps:

The use of the repeated tone and the firm staccato are characteristic of this early work:[49]

---

45. Kalliwoda (1801-1866) studied in Prague. From 1823 to 1853 he was *Kapellmeister* at the court of Donaueschingen, where he achieved a considerable reputation as a versatile composer. His works included symphonies, overtures, masses, and compositions for the violin.

46. R. Schumann, *Gesammelte Schriften über Musik und Musiker* (Second edition, 1871), Vol. II, p. 185.

47. Pablo de Sarasate (1844-1908) won first prize at the Paris Conservatoire in 1857, and became widely acclaimed as a virtuoso. His violin compositions were also much *en vogue*.

48. Leipzig: Breitkopf und Härtel, orchestra parts.

49. This concerto was published prior to 1828.

The Larghetto, in the lowered mediant key (G), contains figurations and dramatic recitatives that foreshadow the work of Vieuxtemps;[50] while some of the technical idioms in the Rondo anticipate those of Sarasate.[51]

The orchestral accompaniment of the concerto includes the following instrumentation:

2 flutes	2 horns
2 oboes	2 trumpets
2 clarinets	tympani
2 bassoons	strings

WILHELM BERNHARD MOLIQUE[52]

Like others representative of the virtuoso concerto, Molique had little formal training in musical composition; nevertheless, he became a prolific and versatile writer, creating works of rather solid musical content. He composed seven violin concertos,[53] of which No. V, in A minor, opus 21,[54] is the best known. Its coherent form and motive structures divulge a skillful compositional technique.

50. This resemblance is also evident in the Larghetto of Kalliwoda's Concertino No. IV, opus 100.

51. See Sarasate's *Introduction and Tarantelle* for Violin and Pianoforte.

52. Molique (1802-1869) was born in Nürnberg. His studying was done with Spohr and Rovelli. After holding positions in Vienna, Munich, and Stuttgart, he settled in London, where he enjoyed great prestige as a soloist, quartet player, and pedagogue.

53. The Seventh Concerto was apparently never published. See F. Schröder, *Bernhard Molique und seine Instrumentalkompositionen*, pp. 106, 111.

54. Leipzig: Hofmeister, original edition revised by J. Dont and H. Schradieck, pianoforte score and orchestra parts.

The first movement of this concerto begins with an orchestral exposition (104 measures) in which fragmentary material is predominant. Theme I contains an essential motive:

Theme II (meas. 172) commences in the sub-mediant key (F major) and modulates to the mediant (C). In the reprise it begins in D and modulates to A major. Such modulations within the course of a theme are peculiar to Molique's writing. In the development there are linear concepts that exceed the superficial manipulations observed in some of the earlier concertos reviewed in this chapter. Some of the violin idioms are curiously archaic:

Other idioms reflect the influence of Spohr, especially the free embellishments and chromaticism of the Andante.

The prolix Rondo begins with an introduction of nine measures preceding a stiff main theme, after which follow:

Theme II (meas. 107) in the mediant key
Theme I (meas. 197)
Theme III (meas. 237)
Theme II
Cadenza (improvised by the soloist)
Coda

There are also various intervening episodes.

The scoring of Concerto No. V consists of a single flute, pairs of wood-winds, trumpets, horns, together with tympani and strings. The instrumentation is noteworthy because of the emancipation of the violoncello part from that of the contrabass. This is, perhaps, a result of the composer's special interest in the violoncello.[55]

HEINRICH WILHELM ERNST[56]

Ernst was particularly admired by Schumann[57] and Joachim; and Andreas Moser termed him ". . . the most brilliant virtuoso since Paganini." His style of writing has a fervent and dramatic quality. The melos is rich, and the passages are extraordinarily difficult. But the compositions are of unequal value, and they reflect the dominant and sometimes derogatory influence of Paganini and De Bériot.[58]

The Concerto in F-sharp minor, opus 23,[59] is unusual in the realm of the violin concerto, for it has but one movement, Allegro pathétique.[60] After a protracted orchestral exposition (98 measures), the solo violin begins with a recitative over the dominant chord. The announcement of the first theme (meas. 104) is dramatic and impassioned:

55. Molique wrote a Concerto for Violoncello and Orchestra, opus 45.

56. Ernst (1814-1865) was a pupil of Mayseder and Böhm. As a youth, he heard Paganini and became so enraptured with the latter's virtuosity that he followed him in his travels. Ultimately Ernst became a formidable rival of the celebrated Italian violinist.

57. Schumann reviewed Ernst's concert in Leipzig (January 14, 1840) in terms of high praise.—*Gesammelte Schriften*, Vol. III, pp. 208-210.

58. Charles A. de Bériot (1802-1870) was a distinguished Belgian violinist and pedagogue. His violin compositions were instructive and occasionally difficult.

59. Leipzig: Peters (revised by A. Hilf). Ricordi and Breitkopf und Härtel editions were also used. Other well known violin compositions by Ernst are *Fantasia* on airs from Rossini's *Otello*, opus 11; *Concertino* in D major, opus 12; *Hungarian Airs*, opus 22; and *Rondo Papageno*, opus 30.

60. The author has never seen any evidence of additional movements for this concerto. The formal structure appears, therefore, to resemble that of Concertos Nos. I and IV, opera 16 and 46, by De Bériot, and, to a lesser extent, Concerto, opus 22, by Goetz. For information on the latter, see *infra*, pp. 91-92.

A phrase from the second theme manifests the composer's gift for lyrical melody:

A long development (meas. 236) reveals adept thematic manipulations and a brilliant array of pyrotechnical effects for the solo instrument. The reprise commences with the second theme (meas. 366) in the parallel major key (F-sharp). Theme I, however, does not return. In measure 420 a Lento recitative (10 measures) is interposed as the solo violin and horn answer one another with a motive. A grandiose climax (meas. 442) is reached at the juncture at which a phrase from the second theme recurs in octaves in the high registers of the solo instrument. A terse coda (Allegro molto) concludes the movement. There is a highly advanced double-stop technique:

This G-string arpeggio recalls Paganini's bravura style:

The accompaniment is scored for

2 flutes	3 horns
2 oboes	2 trumpets
2 clarinets	3 trombones
2 bassoons	tympani

strings

FERDINAND DAVID [61]

A lexicon, dating from 1856, terms David's compositions for his instrument ". . . among the finest in the entire literature. . . ."[62] A more recent author, however, is less extravagant in his evaluation of David's merits when he states that ". . . his compositions reveal a thorough musical knowledge united with charming melodic invention and rhythmic piquancy. . . ."[63]

The first movement (Allegro serioso) of Concerto No. V in D minor, opus 35,[64] is especially interesting because of the concentrative and varied presentations of a single motive. This particular technique had been utilized effectively by Mendelssohn in his Violin Concerto, opus 64.[65] The important motive (X) is contained in the main theme:

61. David (1810-1873) was a pupil of Spohr and Hauptmann. In 1827 he made the acquaintance of Mendelssohn—a circumstance that proved to be a turning point in his career. It was due to Mendelssohn's influence that David was appointed concertmaster of the *Gewandhaus* Orchestra in Leipzig nine years later. In that role, and also as a quartet player and pedagogue, he soon achieved fame. Among his pupils were Joachim and Wilhelmj. David's violin compositions included five concertos and a number of miscellaneous pieces. He also transcribed various works by Classical masters. His potent influence on the composition of the Mendelssohn Violin Concerto, opus 64, will be discussed in Chapter IV.

62. E. Bernsdorf (Hsg.), *Neues Universal-Lexikon der Tonkunst,* Vol. I, p. 660.

63. P. Stoeving, *Von der Violine,* p. 255.

64. Breitkopf und Härtel, pianoforte score.   65. See *infra,* pp. 70-71.

It becomes inverted in measures 42-43, 124-125, 154-155, and in other measures. It is augmented in the announcement by the solo violin, beginning the solo exposition:

Further manipulations of the motive are disclosed in the following presentation embracing both augmentation and inversion:

and in the modified canonical version of measures 208-209:

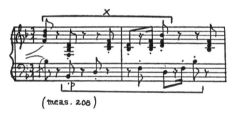

Subsequently, with the commencement of the reprise (meas. 251), motive X recurs in its original form but in a low register.

The principal keys of this ingenious movement are

D minor (meas. 1)	theme I
D minor (meas. 54)	theme I
F major (meas. 112)	theme II
B-flat major (meas. 194)	theme I
D minor (meas. 251)	theme I
A major (meas. 277)	theme II

D major (meas. 341) . . . . . . theme I
D minor (meas. 369) . . . . . . coda

It is indeed curious that August Wilhelmj in his freely revised
edition of this concerto used the above movement as his finale,
and substituted another first movement that was evidently not
David's own. Such freedom cannot be condoned, especially when
it distorts the organic unity of the work as a whole.

A lyrical melody in the second movement (Adagio)[66]

is restated in a brief Adagio section of the Finale vivace (meas.
345-349), thus providing a cyclical link. The Finale vivace bears
further evidence of the *principe cyclique,* as motive X from the
first movement[67] returns in an Allegro moderato section immediately preceding the Vivace (coda). The organic unity of this
rondo is also perceptible in the rhythmic and thematic similarities
of the contrasting sections beginning in measures 96 and 188,
respectively. The principal theme of the Finale is quoted:

Wilhelmj discarded this entire movement in his distorted revision
of the concerto.

SUMMARY

Some of the early Romanticists, notably Bohrer, Böhm, Mayseder, Maurer, Kalliwoda, and Lipinski, were, like Spohr, products
of the Napoleonic and Metternich eras. Others, for example,
Molique, Ernst, and David, may be said to represent the more

66. A brief recitative on the dominant ninth chord immediately preceding the
close of this movement is the only semblance of a cadenza in the entire concerto.
  67. See *supra,* p. 58.

individualistic spirit typified by the political upheavals of 1830 and 1848.

Although these composers frequently utilized formal constructions that were prescriptive and stereotyped, they gave us, nevertheless, some indications of freedom in the application of musical designs. Ernst, for example, conceived a violin concerto in one movement; Maurer used occasional recitatives; and several composers either omitted a theme from the reprise, or reversed the order of the themes in the reprise. David dispensed with the formal cadenza, and, like Mendelssohn, he employed a concentrative motive technique that foreshadowed Bruch, Goldmark, and Brahms. He also made an effort to weld the concerto into an organic whole by interposing motives from the first and second movements of his Concerto, opus 35, in the finale. This cyclical procedure was anticipative of similar experiments by Goetz and Bruch.

The virtuosic composers were myopic, for they exaggerated the predominance of the solo violin part and the importance of pyrotechnical effects. They were, however, remarkable in their development of violin technique. The compositions of Paganini, Lipinski, and Ernst were pre-eminent in this connection. The inheritance of specific technical idioms from Viotti, Rode, and Kreutzer was observed particularly in the works of Bohrer, Böhm, Mayseder, and Maurer.

Maurer, together with Molique, followed trends that had been marked by Spohr. Thus Molique was affected by Spohr's chromaticism; and Maurer emulated his recitative types. Maurer's adaptation of folk tunes to the violin concerto was significant in that it anteceded the nationalistic movement in the later music of the nineteenth century.

Another striking trait is the thoroughly *melodic* conception of these concertos. The composers were violinists, and therefore went back to the nature of the instrument itself for their ingratiating melodies. Thus they stood in direct contrast with the *harmonic* conceptions of many subsequent writers who thought, almost exclusively, in terms of pianoforte idioms.

Although the instrumentation of these concertos was marked by an enlargement of the brass choir, it was otherwise archaic and effete.

JAKOB LUDWIG FELIX MENDELSSOHN-BARTHOLDY[1]

W HEN Mendelssohn was but twelve years old, his theory instructor, C. F. Zelter, introduced him to Goethe, and a friendship between the famous old philosopher and the youthful musician soon developed. Mendelssohn later referred to this in a letter from Weimar: "Goethe is so friendly and kind to me that I scarcely know how to thank him. In the morning, I must play the piano for him, about an hour from the works of all the great composers arranged chronologically; and then I must tell him how they all have progressed. In the meantime, he sits in a dark corner like a Jupiter *tonans* with his old eyes sparkling."[2] Also exceptionally fortunate for his early development was his contact with other intellectuals and artists, such as Hegel, Heine, Moscheles, and Lindblad, who visited his home as guests of the family.

In 1829 Mendelssohn began his extensive European travels. In 1835 he became conductor of the celebrated *Gewandhaus* Orchestra in Leipzig, and later (1843) he founded the Leipzig *Konserva-*

1. Felix Mendelssohn (1809-1847) was the son of a Jewish banker, Abraham Mendelssohn. The latter, in 1823, secured the permission of the government to attach the name Bartholdy to his own family name in the light of his conversion to Protestant Christianity.

2. *Reisebriefe aus den Jahren 1830 bis 1832,* hsg. von Paul Mendelssohn-Bartholdy (Fifth edition), Vol. I, p. 8. The letter was dated May 25, 1830.

torium. Among his collaborators in this undertaking were David, Schumann, and Hauptmann. The remaining years of his versatile career as a composer, conductor, and pianist were spent mainly in Germany and England.

His happy family life, inspiring friendships with some of the most distinguished men of the time, and his financial independence contributed to fashion a career of almost incomparable felicity. "Few instances can be found in history of a man so amply gifted with every good quality of mind and heart; so carefully brought up amongst good influences; endowed with every circumstance that would make him happy; and so thoroughly fulfilling his mission."[3]

Mendelssohn, like Mozart, displayed a prodigious talent for composition while he was very young. When he was seventeen years of age, he composed the Overture to *Midsummer Night's Dream,* an epochal work of great imagination and originality. This was really a crucial turning point in his artistic development, for his inner nature and individuality had now definitely asserted themselves.

It was from Bach, Händel, Haydn, and Mozart that Mendelssohn inherited his profound appreciation of the Classical forms; and it is not surprising, therefore, that his works are characterized by a remarkable organic unity. He linked together the movements of his Violin Concerto, opus 64, and utilized a cohesive motive technique. In harmonic texture Mendelssohn was a master of consonance. The gamut of his emotional experience was somewhat limited, and he was never able to attain the profundity of Beethoven and Brahms. Nevertheless, his art is distinguished for its perspicuity, charm, Romantic humor, and exuberance.

It is certainly a provocative matter for musicologists to learn that Mendelssohn composed an early violin concerto, the manuscript of which rests in the possession of the Preussische Staatsbib-

3. G. Grove, "Mendelssohn," in *Grove's Dictionary of Music and Musicians* (Third edition, 1935), Vol. III, p. 428.

liothek in Berlin. The work is ostensibly scored for string quartet. Professor Schünemann, in a letter to the author, submits the following information: "We are not concerned here with a matured work, but rather with a school task which he wrote along with many other concertos, when he was but fourteen years old. . . . The piece *never* exceeded the prescriptive limitations of school work." The themes of the movements are given:

Mendelssohn's Concerto for Violin and Orchestra in E minor, opus 64,[4] is an outstanding achievement in Romantic music and continues to hold its place with the concertos of Beethoven and Brahms. The manuscript of this concerto was completed at Bad Soken, near Frankfurt am Main, and was dated September 16, 1844. It was published during the following year.

Like Brahms with Joachim, it was essential for Mendelssohn to solicit the aid of a violinist. In a letter to his friend, Ferdinand David, dated December 17, 1844, the composer mentions that he had just sent the score to Breitkopf und Härtel, and that he had made several changes which he hoped would be improvements. Then he continues: "I should like your opinion on all these matters before I hand on the work, irrevocably, to the public."[5]

The violinist, in a subsequent communication, wrote: ". . . That you are not opposed to the changes in (your) Violin Concerto

4. Breitkopf und Härtel, Gesamtausgabe, Serie IV.
5. J. Eckardt, *Ferdinand David und die Familie Mendelssohn-Bartholdy*, p. 224.

pleases me very much. I have entered them in the solo part, which you will see again before publication. I have also made other revisions and taken out superfluous fingerings and bowings, and added new ones. You should eliminate all superfluities."[6]

In another letter Mendelssohn said: "How good of you to have fulfilled my request, and to have occupied yourself with my Concerto! I am sincerely grateful for your suggestions. . . ."[7]

The first performance of the concerto took place in a *Gewandhaus* concert on March 13, 1845. David was the soloist and Niels Gade, the conductor.[8] The performance evoked the following comments: "David afforded us the greatest pleasure in the last concert of the season . . . through his masterful performance of the Mendelssohn Violin Concerto, which is to us the finest composition for this instrument since Beethoven and Spohr."[9]

David wrote to Mendelssohn about the première: "I should have informed you long ago of the success with which I first publicly performed your Violin Concerto. . . . It won extraordinary favor, and was unanimously declared to be one of the finest works of its kind. It fulfills to the highest degree all demands that one might make of a concert piece; and violinists cannot be sufficiently grateful to you for this gift. Above everything, I must thank you for the privilege of introducing such a work to the public . . . of which I am not a little proud. . . . Everyone agreed that the solo violin was heard clearly at all times, even in the heaviest orchestrated places. . . . May the great success of this work so please you that you will again think of us forlorn violinists."[10]

---

6. *Ibid.*, p. 229, a letter from Leipzig, dated January 2, 1845.

7. *Ibid.*, pp. 229-230.

8. Other performances soon followed: October 23, with David again as the soloist; and November 10, in Dresden, with Joachim as soloist. See T. Müller-Reuter, *Lexikon der deutschen Konzertliteratur*, Nachtrag zu Bd. I, p. 88.

9. W. Lampadius, *Felix Mendelssohn-Bartholdy*, p. 316.

10. A letter from David to Mendelssohn, dated March 27, 1845.—Eckardt, *Ferdinand David und die Familie Mendelssohn-Bartholdy*, pp. 232-233.

ANALYSIS

The Allegro molto appassionato is a consummate example of the sonata form. The orchestral exposition is omitted, thus causing the form to be identical with that generally used for the opening movement of a sonata. The *innig* and expressive first theme, with its significant motives and figures,

appears after one and one-half measures of undulating accompaniment figures in the violins and violas:

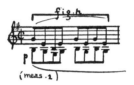

These figures are important because of their function as cohesive "joints" for other sections in the movement. An awkward passage in octaves on a diminished seventh chord is conspicuous because of its difficulty:

A variation of this passage begins in measure 44. These and similar passages[11] demand exceptional accuracy of intonation.

In measure 47 the orchestra takes up the pronouncement of the first theme, but soon relinquishes it for new episodical material. The most attractive and important of these episodes (N)

---

11. Note the chromatic octave series in the coda (meas. 455-458).

occurs after a cadence in the tonic key. Note its reappearance in measures 226-262, 351-373, and 473-520.

The application of a diminutive musical figure is typical of the composer's concentrative style:

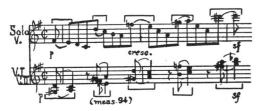

After vehement declamatory passages in the solo part (meas. 113-130), we are prepared for the announcement of the second theme in the relative major key (G). The antecedent phrase is given to the first clarinet, while the solo violin clings to a tonic pedal point:

The solo violin takes up the theme in measure 139. This leads to one of the most graceful and "feminine" effects of the entire movement (meas. 165) as the natural harmonic *a* is quitted by means of a soft downward portamento.

The development (meas. 168) reverts to the beginning of the movement with a presentation of the first phrase of theme I, accompanied by the familiar eight-note undulations. Extraneous figures in the solo part appear against motive Z in the accompaniment (meas. 173-181):

The pianistic figurations in the succeeding measures of the solo violin part reappear in the coda. In measure 199 figure *u* prevails in the flute and oboe parts. A powerful climax is reached (meas. 208-218) with the pompous declamations in the solo violin. Episode N returns (meas. 226); and a diminution of figure *x* is presently set forth in tenuous passages that provide the accompaniment for motive Y, in the wood-winds:

The cadenza is anticipated as figure h^{12} recurs in measures 255-297. Observe, also, the extensions of motive Y in the solo violin part (meas. 262-289) and in the first violin and oboe parts (meas. 290-298). In measure 290 there are agitated tremolos in the tympani as a puissant crescendo rises. The "Cadenza ad libitum" makes its appearance in measure 299:

12. See *supra*, p. 66.

*This *f-sharp* is played as a unison, so as to enable the performer to execute the tonal pattern on four strings, as in the preceding measure. This slight modification was advocated by Kneisel and Auer.

In writing out his own cadenza, Mendelssohn adopted a procedure that was subsequently utilized by Joachim, Goldmark, Sibelius, and other composers. Another interesting feature is that the cadenza here constitutes a link between the development and the reprise.

The reprise commences in a subtle manner as the first theme enters (meas. 335), pianissimo, in the first flute, first oboe, and first violins following a diminuendo in the *ricochet* arpeggios of the solo violin. A powerful crescendo leads to a full cadence in the tonic key (meas. 351), after which episode N reasserts itself in the orchestra. Theme II returns in the tonic major key (meas. 377). Subsequently (meas. 401), one of its phrases is accompanied by a mellifluous counterpoint in the solo violin part:

The psychological effect of the D-sharp minor diminished seventh chord (meas. 418), inaugurating the coda, is dynamic. The coda is distinctive because of its impressive dimensions and detailed treatment. After a definitive cadence in the tonic minor key (meas. 473), episode N recurs persistently until the close of the movement; and the tempo is accelerated to Più presto and Presto. The tone *b*, from the final cadence chord, is sustained in the bassoon part for two measures, and functions as a pivotal and connecting link to the ensuing movement.

The Andante is one of the purest expressions in Romantic music. Its form is ternary: A — B — A — coda. An unobtrusive introduction establishes the key of C major (meas. 5). The first part consists of a double period (18 measures) followed by a series of related phrases. An excerpt from the felicitous melody is quoted:

An interesting harmonic idiom occurs in the following example, in which the tone *c* serves as a cadence pedal, in the manner of Spohr:[13]

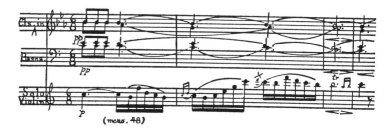

(meas. 48)

In the second part (meas. 52) the orchestra enunciates a contrasting motive with vital accompaniment figurations:

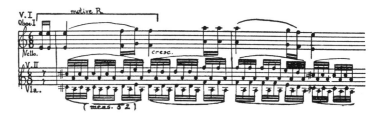

(meas. 52)

A derivative of this motive is used in the Allegretto non troppo commencing the third movement.[14] Thus it serves as a connecting link in the coherent organism of the whole. The solo violin now takes up motive R (meas. 55), accompanying itself by the thirty-second-note figures. A crescendo ensues, after which (meas. 61) the accompaniment figures and motive fragments are shifted about so as to give antiphonal effects between the orchestra and solo violin. The harmony in this section is characterized by profuse transient modulations, although the principal tonalities remain A minor and D minor.

The key of C major is reached with the cadence in measure 79 for the return of the first part. The thirty-second-note figurations

13. See *supra*, pp. 14-15.   14. See *infra*, p. 71.

provide an overlapping link (meas. 78-79); and there is an incomparable *Stimmungszauber* as part two fades into a tenuous pianissimo before and with the recurrence of part 1 and the principal melody (meas. 76-79). A brief coda (meas. 99) provides a graceful close.

It will be recalled that the third movement (Allegretto non troppo—Allegro molto vivace) was connected to the Andante by a manipulation of motive R:

The key of E minor is used for this transitional section. Special emphasis is given the dominant chord (meas. 8-14) in preparation for the long Allegro molto vivace. At the commencement of the latter (meas. 15), the key changes to the parallel major (E). The Allegro molto vivace has a free rondo form: A — B — C — A — B — coda. A signal motive in the bassoons, horns, and trumpets is accompanied by a vigorous tremolo in the tympani:

This is answered by a scintillating figure in the solo violin:

The first theme suggests a roguish play,

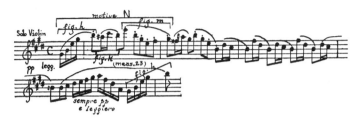

and has a Romantic humor that is also characteristic of the composer's Overture to *Midsummer Night's Dream*. Note, especially, figures *h, k,* and *m,* contained within motive N. In measure 51 there begins a passage that requires exceptional dexterity in the shifting of positions:

After a fortissimo scale over an F-sharp seventh chord (meas. 67), the second theme makes its appearance in the key of the dominant (B major):

Motive S is of vital importance.

Following a cadence in the dominant key (meas. 95), a developmental section begins with prankish *sautillé* passages in the solo part, against which are reproductions of motive S in the orchestra. In measure 115 the first phrase of theme I reasserts itself in the solo violin (G major). Subsequently (meas. 121), the principal motive and figures are applied to the orchestral strings while the solo violin enunciates theme III:

In measure 131 the solo part takes up motive N and cognate figures, while the violins, violas, and violoncellos (meas. 132) present an altered version of theme III. Note, also, the key change to B major. A transitional passage in the solo violin (meas. 141-146) demands absolute control of the flying staccato:

The restatement of theme I, in the solo violin part, begins in measure 146. A phrase from theme III (first violins, violas, violoncellos) forms a counterpoint against it. This thematic section is abbreviated by twenty-nine measures. The heavily accentuated second theme (meas. 164) is transposed to the tonic major key. This section is also abbreviated, being eighteen measures shorter than its original pronouncement. A working-over of motive S and its fragments (meas. 182) is enhanced by the filigree *sautillé* passages. This is reminiscent of the developmental middle section.

In measure 197 a trill cadenza and a recitative intervene before the beginning of the coda (meas. 216). Powerful unison passages culminate in a high *e* (meas. 232) in the solo violin; and the movement leads to a buoyant close.

The orchestral accompaniment includes:

2 flutes	2 trumpets
2 oboes	2 horns
2 clarinets	tympani
2 bassoons	strings

A very conservative trait is noted in the persistent doubling of the violoncello and contrabass parts. On the other hand, the symphonic participation of the orchestra is advanced and significant. The instrumentation is also eminently practicable.

BETWEEN MENDELSSOHN
and BRAHMS

W ITH but two exceptions, the violin concertos reviewed in this chapter were published between 1860 and 1885. The following German composers are represented: Schumann, Joachim, Raff, Hellmesberger, Goetz, Reinecke, Bruch, Hiller, Damrosch, Goldmark, Dietrich, Gernsheim, Brüll, Rüfer, Sitt, and Strauss.

This historical epoch was characterized by a series of momentous political changes: the ascendancy of Bismarck, the Austro-Prussian War, the Franco-Prussian War, the rise of unified empires in Germany and Italy, and the struggles of democracy and socialism. The amazing scientific and industrial developments were also effecting dynamic changes in the life of Europe.

In philosophy the influence of Hegel and Schopenhauer was being gradually superseded by that of the Neo-Kantians and Nietzsche. In literature new personalities such as Hugo, Flaubert, Zola, Tennyson, Browning, Thackeray, Dickens, Rossetti, Ibsen, Björnson, and Heyse were pre-eminent. In art the Impressionists were beginning to declare their new esthetic creed. Form, they insisted, was not design but coherence; and only that which was "beautiful" was correct. In music the dominance of the early

Romanticists was counteracted by Liszt, Wagner, Verdi, and Brahms.

The composers of the violin concerto during this era minimized the virtuosic trends that were conspicuous in many of the earlier concertos and sought to achieve an expression on a different musical niveau. Their conceptions, on the whole, were more pianistic than violinistic; their accompaniments, more important; their rhythms, more diverse; and their technique, more concentrative and less uniform.

ROBERT SCHUMANN [1]

Schumann's only violin concerto, according to Professor Schünemann, was composed and orchestrated in less than two weeks— from September 21 to October 3, 1853.[2] Joachim, however, declared in a letter to Moser[3] that the inscription, "Düsseldorf, 11. September, . . . 3. Oktober 1853," appeared on the title page. In any event, the composer promptly acquainted his wife with the concerto, as we may infer from the insertion in her *Tagebuch*

---

1. Schumann (1810-1856) was destined for a law career, attending the universities of Leipzig (1828) and Heidelberg (1829-1830). Subsequently, he relinquished these studies in order to become a musician.

His early compositions were almost exclusively written for the pianoforte; and they were repellent to both musicians and public. "For the great multitude of dilettantes, his compositions were too difficult and incomprehensible; for professional musicians, they were eccentric, and departed too radically from the established rules and traditions."—A. W. Ambros, *Culturhistorische Bilder aus dem Musikleben der Gegenwart* (1865), p. 60. It was not until after the publication of the *Kinderscenen,* opus 15, that Schumann began to win his way into public favor.

After his marriage to Clara Wieck in 1840, he made frequent tours with her, but the center of his activities remained in Leipzig, Dresden, and Düsseldorf.

Schumann's position as a critic was distinguished. He founded the *Neue Zeitschrift für Musik* (1834), in which he asserted himself as a champion of the old Classical masters as well as of the new composers. Among the latter, he admired especially Schubert, Mendelssohn, Chopin, and Brahms. He was captivated by the Romantic spirit of Jean Paul, although he read assiduously the works of Goethe, Shakespeare, Heine, Byron, and Rückert.

2. See preface to the Schott edition of the concerto.

3. The letter is dated August 5, 1898. A facsimile of it is given in A. Moser, *Joseph Joachim,* Vol. I, facing p. 178.

bearing the date October 7, 1853: "Robert has finished a highly interesting violin concerto. He played a little of it for me; yet I dare not say more about it until I have really heard it. The Adagio and the last movement were at once quite clear to me; but the first movement was not entirely so."[4]

On the occasion of Schumann's visit to Hannover at the beginning of the year 1854, Joachim played the work twice for the composer at an orchestral rehearsal. Schumann was so disappointed with it that he undertook his homeward journey to Düsseldorf with the resolution that he must revise the work completely.[5] But this was never done.

After the composer's death, Frau Schumann implored both Joachim and Brahms to make some essential revisions in the concerto. They refused, however, asserting that, even if the experiment did turn out to Clara's satisfaction, the result would not be Schumann's own work.[6] The manuscript was presented by Clara to Joachim, and it remained in his possession until his death in 1907, after which it was acquired by the Preussische Staatsbibliothek in Berlin. It was published in 1937,[7] and the première took place in Berlin on November 26 of that year, when Georg Kulenkampf played it with the Berlin Philharmonic Orchestra.

Joachim's opinion of the composition is evident from the following adverse criticism: "It must be regretfully stated that it betrays a certain decline, from which spiritual (*geistige*) energy tries to free itself. Individual passages, (how could it be otherwise!) give evidence of a profound creative spirit; but the contrast with the work as a whole is all the more disappointing."[8] The violinist also peremptorily stated: "Such a work ought not be printed, or performed in public, since it would add nothing to the composer's laurels!"[9]

---

4. B. Litzmann, *Clara Schumann*, Vol. II, p. 282.
5. Moser, *Joseph Joachim*, Vol. II, p. 374.   6. *Ibid.*
7. London: Schott and Co., Ltd. (2588), pianoforte score by G. Schünemann. Also, Mainz: B. Schott's Söhne, orchestra score.
8. See note 3 in this chapter.   9. Moser, *Joseph Joachim*, Vol. II, p. 374.

Despite its admirable formal unity and poetic musical qualities, the work is stereotyped and ill-suited to the solo instrument because of the cumbrous, unviolinistic idioms. A drastic revision of the orchestral score is also imperative before it can be regarded as a worthy companion piece to Schumann's Concertos for Pianoforte and Orchestra, opus 54, and Violoncello and Orchestra, opus 129.

The first movement of the violin concerto, marked "In kräftigem, nicht zu schnellem Tempo," is repetitious and uneven. It is devoid of contrapuntal textures and has a prolix harmonic background. On the other hand, there is an admirable unity of thematic elements. The sonorous orchestral exposition (53 measures) is the most prominent formal section in the movement. It recurs (either as a whole, or in part) in the solo exposition, development, reprise, and coda. This exposition begins with a pronouncement of the main theme in the first violins and flute (an octave higher):

The above four-measure phrase is given a modified version when it appears in the solo violin part (meas. 54):

A lyrical second theme appears in the orchestral exposition in the relative major key (F):

Joachim described this as ". . . a tender and richly melodious second theme, genuinely Schumannesque!"[10] But he insisted that it was not developed effectively. He believed, moreover, that the succeeding violin passages were awkward and did not afford a brilliant conclusion of the exposition. The composer is said to have altered the following passage because it was unplayable on the violin:

His revision, however, is virtually unplayable as it is written:[11]

The development begins with a transposed but otherwise literal restatement of the first twenty-eight measures of the orchestral exposition. Then follow excerpts from the solo exposition and extensive manipulations of the second theme (meas. 177-216). Figure y is important. Prominent tonalities in the development are F major, G minor, B-flat major, and D minor. The modulations are generally next-related and more conservative than one would expect in a matured work by Schumann. A pungent cross relation is found in measure 126:

10. See note 3 in this chapter.

11. Schott edition (2588); see preface and appendix by G. Schünemann for these and other alterations by the composer.

A pedal point on the dominant of the principal key (meas. 203) leads to a voluminous reprise (meas. 217). Measures 160-220 are hardly fully exploited because the violin register and the instrumentation do not give adequate support to the approaching climax.

In the reprise, thirty measures from the orchestral exposition, dealing with the main theme, are presented before the return of the solo exposition. There is no formal cadenza in any of the movements.

The coda (meas. 318) makes another reference to theme I, with material corresponding to the first twelve measures of the orchestral exposition. The utilization of this same thematic material in the coda, reprise, development, and orchestral exposition makes for the concentrated formal organization of the movement. Figure y (meas. 332) in the viola part is pitted against the oppositional rhythms of the solo part, and seems anticipative of the polyrhythmic structures of Brahms.[12]

Joachim reviewed the second movement as follows: "The second movement (marked 'langsam') commences with tender and profound feeling, and leads to an 'expressive' melody in the violin. If only this felicitous dreaming might continue . . . noble master! So warm, so fervent [innig] . . . as of old! But the imaginative power (how one's heart bleeds to confess it!) yields to weak broodings. The flow is impeded, but winds along thematically somewhat further; and then, as if the composer himself yearns to escape from the dismal cloud of these reflections, he recovers himself with a transition in accelerating tempo to the last movement. . . ."[13]

The second movement is but fifty-three measures long and comprises the following sections: introduction — A — interlude (= introduction) — A' — transition (4 measures) to the finale.
The poetic melody

12. See Brahms' Concerto for Violin and Orchestra, op. 77 (Adagio, meas. 69-70).   13. See note 3 in this chapter.

is enhanced by a syncopated figure in the accompaniment

taken from the first measure of the introduction. This figure
reasserts itself in the finale (meas. 137 et al.). Tonalities stressed
during the course of the movement are

> B-flat major (meas. 1)
> F major (meas. 9)
> C minor (meas. 24)
> B-flat major (meas. 32)
> G minor (meas. 36)
> B-flat major (meas. 50)
> A major (meas. 53)

Observe, also, the chromatic and shifting harmonies (meas. 41-50),
and characteristic pedal effects (meas. 13-18).

Joachim humorously refers to the finale ("Lebhaft, doch nicht
schnell") in a letter to Schumann:[14] "Now the 3-4 time sounds
much more imposing. Do you recall how you laughed as we im-
agined that the last movement sounded as if Kosciuszko[15] were
beginning a Polonaise with Sobiĕski[16] . . . that stately?" In a
frequently quoted letter to Moser,[17] he mentioned a "certain characteristic stiffness of the rhythm" and the prolix, sinuous repeti-

14. Dated November 17, 1854.—Moser, *Joseph Joachim*, Vol. I, p. 213.

15. Kosciuszko (1746-1817) was a Polish general who participated in the Polish
insurrections against Russia in 1794. After his defeat and imprisonment, he resided
in France, Switzerland, and other countries.

16. Sobiĕski was John III, King of Poland from 1674-1696. With his Polish
forces he gained an important victory over the Turks in 1683.

17. See note 3 in this chapter.

tions. He admired, however, the "allusions to the contemplative Adagio" (evidently meas. 137 *et al.*).[18] This finale is linked to the second movement by means of figure *h*.[19] Another salient feature is the heavily accented rhythm in the strings and horns accompanying the pronouncement of the first theme:

The form is a rondo: A (54) — B (72) — transition (135) — A' (156) — A (188) — B (206) — transition and new material (269) — brief episodical references to A (278) — coda (289).

The accompaniment of the concerto is scored for a Classical orchestra with strings, tympani, and pairs of wood-winds, horns and trumpets. The inertia of the orchestral accompaniment appears to be an obvious deficiency. We recall, especially, the unsatisfactory conclusions of the first and third movements, jejune treatment of the trumpet part, and apparent failure to allow a sufficient number of sustaining effects as a substitute for the pianoforte pedal. Nevertheless, the orchestration of the second movement has merit; and that of the finale reveals some effective participation of the wood-wind and brass instruments.

Joseph Joachim[20]

As a child, Joachim had been tremendously impressed by the virtuosity of Heinrich Ernst. By a curious turn of fortune, it was Ernst who took the boy to Joseph Böhm in the Vienna *Konserva-*

18. The first measure of the finale is numbered 54.
19. See second movement (meas. 50-51).
20. Joachim (1831-1907) was born at Kitsee (near Pressburg), Hungary.

torium for further instruction;[21] and from then on, "Everything developed steadily and logically for him like a broad crescendo that finally reaches a majestic organ point."[22]

At the age of twelve, Joachim made his debut in a Leipzig *Gewandhaus* concert under Mendelssohn's direction, playing the *Otello Fantasie* by Ernst. Six years later he was appointed concertmaster in the orchestra of the Grand Duke of Weimar. As Liszt was then residing in Weimar, it was not long before the young violinist became an enthusiastic member of the Liszt circle. Joachim left Weimar for Hannover in 1853, and from that time on, the influence of the Liszt group ceased to dominate his artistic creed. At the outbreak of the Austro-Prussian War he moved to Berlin, where, two years later, he began his illustrious career in the newly founded *Königliche Hochschule*.

As a virtuoso and chamber music player, Joachim was a paramount figure in the musical world of the nineteenth century. More than any other artist, perhaps, he was responsible for consummate traditional interpretations of masters such as Bach, Haydn, Mozart, Beethoven, Spohr, Schubert, Mendelssohn, and Schumann. His influence on contemporary composers was of tremendous import; for the violin concertos by Mendelssohn, Schumann, Gade, Reinecke, Bruch, Hiller, Damrosch, Brahms, and Dvořák were either written for him or else directly inspired by him.

Among Joachim's early compositions were a number of violin and symphonic works. The former included the Violin Concerto in G minor, opus 3, and the better known *Hungarian* Concerto, opus 11. The Concerto in G minor, in one movement, was conceived in the Liszt *Geistesrichtung*. In later years it was seldom played by the composer because he believed the work was not representative of his matured artistic trends. The *Hungarian* Concerto in D minor, opus 11,[23] was written in 1854 and dedicated to Johannes Brahms. It was the product of influences which Joachim

21. Moser, *Joseph Joachim*, Vol. I, p. 26.   22. *Ibid.*, p. 90.
23. Leipzig: Breitkopf und Härtel, orchestra and pianoforte scores.

owed to the national music of his native land. The varied impressions of his youth ". . . could only strengthen him in his predilection for the distinctive melodies, harmonies, and rhythms of the Magyar folk songs and dances."[24]

We have already referred to the nationalistic trend in early Romantic music with examples from Spohr and Maurer,[25] and we know that it represents one of the vital musical developments of the nineteenth century. Joachim's use of sensuous folk melodies in his *Hungarian* Concerto was supplemented by a virtuosic conception of technical effects and a profusion of embellishments reminiscent of Spohr. The concerto is serious and excessively long, and it does not merit the extraordinary praise which the composer's biographer bestows upon it: "Aside from its treatment of the violin, it is, in its architectonic construction, in its wealth and originality of invention, in its captivating and sensuous melos, and in the wonderful tone-coloring of the orchestral accompaniment . . . far more a work of genius than the Violin Concerto and even the Double Concerto for Violin and Violoncello by Brahms."[26] Such declarations illustrate the evolution of taste during the progress of time.

The Allegro un poco maestoso, which Brahms once termed "wunderschön," is a virtuosic movement that begins with an orchestral exposition of 100 measures. The main theme has a strong Hungarian flavor,

24. Moser, *Joseph Joachim*, Vol. II, p. 83.

25. See *supra*, pp. 17, 48. Many other familiar examples may be found in the works of Liszt, Brahms, Tschaikowsky, Dvořák, Gade, Grieg, Lalo, De Falla, Ravel, and Bartók.   26. Moser, *Joseph Joachim*, Vol. II, pp. 243-244.

with its plaintive mood, "gypsy" minor scale, syncopations, and grace-notes. The rhythmic patterns ♪♩ and ♫ frequently used during the course of the movement, are favorite Hungarian idioms especially adaptable to tonal repetitions. In writing out the cadenza, the composer followed a procedure utilized by Mendelssohn, Bruch, Goldmark, Dietrich, and Gernsheim.

The Romanze (Andante) evoked the following comment from Brahms in a letter to Joachim: "I like your Adagio very much. There is such charm and friendliness in it. The whole flows along so tranquilly and one part evolves from the other so beautifully that it is a joy. In January, I shall hear the entire work. How I am looking forward to it. You are making excellent progress!"[27]

The form of the Romanze is ternary. After an introduction of ten measures, a Magyar melody with suggestive rhythms is enunciated by the solo violin and accompanied by the muted strings and horn:

In the contrasting second part there are imposing double-stops and florid passages in the solo violin against a conspicuous iambic rhythm in the accompaniment. With the return of the first part (meas. 61), the principal melody appears in the violoncellos and first horn, while the solo violin unfolds its profuse embellish-

27. A. Moser (Hsg.), *Johannes Brahms im Briefwechsel mit Joseph Joachim,* Vol. I, pp. 219-220. The letter was dated December 7, 1858. Although Brahms refers here to an Adagio, there is little doubt that he had in mind the slow movement of the *Hungarian* Concerto.—See also *ibid.,* Vol. I, p. 187.

ments. Motive K, borrowed from the first movement,[28] provides a tranquil *Ausklang* in the last seven measures of the coda.

The Finale alla zingara (Allegro) may be regarded as a precursor of the Allegro moderato à la zingara of Wieniawski's Concerto in D minor, opus 22. It is a voluminous rondo with the design: A — B — C — A — D — A — B — C — coda. An ostinato rhythm in the accompaniment supports a swift and rhapsodical main theme:

Does it not appear that the solo part should be moved forward by one beat, so that the expressive accent would correspond with the metrical accent? Section D, a rather large middle part, contains a mellifluous theme (meas. 282) in the sub-mediant major key; and a fiery Presto concludes the movement.

The concerto is replete with difficult and complex violin idioms. A passage in chromatic octaves from the first movement is quoted:

A long trill series in the same movement (meas. 303-310) is complemented by an essential motive in the orchestra, and reminds us of a similar passage in the Beethoven Violin Concerto, opus 61.[29]

28. See *supra*, p. 84.
29. See Allegro ma non troppo (meas. 205-216).

The orchestra accompaniment of the concerto is not significant, despite its full scoring:

2 flutes	4 horns
2 oboes	2 trumpets
2 clarinets	tympani
2 bassoons	strings

Joachim composed his Third Concerto, in G major, during the year 1864. The work was ultimately revised and then published twenty years later. Moser extolled it in these terms: "The G major Concerto cannot be too enthusiastically recommended to violinists who are musically and technically capable of mastering it."[30]

JOSEPH JOACHIM RAFF [31]

When Raff journeyed to Weimar in 1850, he was already a champion of the New German (Liszt) School. He accepted the programmatic ideal. Despite a sentimental and redundant style, he was a good melodist; and his pianistic conceptions indicate that he was adept in the use of varied harmonic textures. His prolific output of instrumental works includes two Concertos for Violin and Orchestra: opus 161, in B minor;[32] and opus 206, in A minor.[33]

The Concerto in A minor was composed in Wiesbaden during the summer of 1877. It was first performed during that year at Erfurt, with Hugo Heermann as soloist.[34] The work is programmatic and in the Liszt *Geistesrichtung*. A poem by Arnold Börner prefaces the concerto:

30. Moser, *Joseph Joachim*, Vol. II, p. 91.

31. Raff (1822-1882) was born in Lachen, on Lake Zürich. Despite circumstances of poverty, he developed into a reputable composer, and achieved an unusual success with instrumental works.

32. Concerto No. I, in B minor, opus 161, was composed in Wiesbaden during the Franco-Prussian War. It was performed there in 1871 with A. Wilhelmj as soloist. The publication of the pianoforte score and orchestra parts dates from the same year.

33. Leipzig: C. F. W. Siegel, orchestra and pianoforte scores. The orchestral score of this concerto was published in 1878.

34. Müller-Reuter, *Lexikon der deutschen Konzertliteratur*, Vol. I, p. 405.

I

Dein Lebensschifflein siehst du schwanken,
Es peitschen Stürme seine Flanken,
Und fruchtlos stemmet ihrer Wuth
Entgegen sich dein frommer Muth.

II

Des Trost's, der Hoffnung lindes Wehen,
Es naht sich dir aus ferner Höhen.
Du fühlst dich wieder kraftdurchglüht
Und Ruhe zieht in dein Gemüth.

III

Scheint auch der Sturm sich neu zu regen:
Du achtest nicht auf sein Bewegen;
Denn was dein Herz mit Leid beschwert,
Ist nun in Freud' und Lust gekehrt.

The opening Allegro has a pianistic conception. An orchestral introduction of sixty-four measures is dominated by a motive,

which is important because of its subsequent adaptation in the finale. Theme I is presented by the solo violin over a syncopated accompaniment in the strings:

The symmetrical phraseology is typical of the composer's writing. The employment of a pedal tone (*e*) in the first announcement of the principal theme is an anomaly in the violin concertos of this period. In the reprise (meas. 343) the second theme precedes the first theme; and a long coda (meas. 443) summarizes the essential thematic material. Except for a few measures in both this movement and the concluding Allegro, there is no formal cadenza.

The second movement, Adagio, is a dignified piece with sensuous melodies and double-stops. The orchestral accompaniment in the first and third parts is marked by a substantial thematic participation of the wood-wind instruments.

The cyclical principle is definitely suggested in the long concluding Allegro, since measures 1-8 and 21-24 correspond, respectively, with measures 1-8 and 25-28 of the first movement. These sections are introductory and involve motive N. This motive is also utilized as a nucleus of the main theme (A major):

Another distinctive formal trait of the finale is the use of the sonata form instead of the customary rondo form.

The accompaniment is scored for

2 flutes	4 horns
2 oboes	2 trumpets
2 clarinets	tympani
2 bassoons	strings

The orchestration is conventional in spirit, but well-equalized and efficacious.

JOSEPH HELLMESBERGER[35]

This composer merits some attention because of his completing the fragment of a Violin Concerto in C major by Beethoven.[36]

35. Joseph Hellmesberger (1828-1893) was the son and pupil of the distinguished pedagogue, Georg Hellmesberger. He became a professor at the Vienna *Konservatorium,* and concertmaster of the Vienna Court Orchestra.

36. The concerto is dedicated to Dr. G. von Breuning. The manuscript is now

This little known early work is provocative from a historical viewpoint.

Beethoven himself composed but 259 measures of the opening movement, and Hellmesberger continued the composition, quite in Beethoven's early style. The orchestral exposition begins with a Mozartian first theme:

Beethoven wrote only as far as 33 measures of the development. From that point Hellmesberger continued the movement by "extending" the leaps (with which Beethoven had left off) up to the recurrence of the principal motive:

The reprise (meas. 325) sets forth the main theme, fortissimo, in the orchestra. No more than one movement of this concerto appears to have been written.

The instrumentation comprises:

1 flute	2 trumpets
2 oboes	tympani
2 bassoons	violins I and II
2 horns	violas I and II
"basso" (violoncellos and contrabasses)	

The omission of the clarinets avows the early origin of this movement, probably about 1800.

---

in the possession of the Gesellschaft der Musikfreunde in Vienna. The orchestra score was published between 1874 and 1879 by F. Schreiber of Vienna, and later reprinted in Schiedermair's *Der Junge Beethoven*.

HERMANN GOETZ[37]

The Concerto in G major, opus 22,[38] by Goetz, is a lyrical and pianistic work in one movement. Taken as a whole, it appears to have a large ternary design: A — B — A — cadenza — coda. Despite the fact that there are no pauses between its well-defined sections, this unique composition may be conveniently analyzed in separate movements, suggested by the tempos indicated: (1) Allegro vivace, (2) Andante, (3) Tempo des ersten Satzes, and (4) Vivace scherzando.

The Allegro vivace (in 12-8 meter) has no orchestral exposition. Instead, there is an orchestral introduction of four measures which precedes the announcement of the main theme in the solo part:

Following the presentation of the subordinate theme and development section, the movement proceeds directly into the Andante (B-flat major). At the conclusion of the latter there is an Ancor' un poco più lento, quasi recit. (9 measures) leading into the Tempo des ersten Satzes, which is a reproduction of the Allegro vivace, but with expansive modifications. Both themes from the Allegro vivace return in the tonic key (G), and the development ultimately leads to a violin cadenza. The cadenza (30 measures) is written out by the composer and serves as a transition to the Vivace scherzando (in 2-4 meter). The thematic material of the latter section is obviously generated from the Allegro vivace.

---

37. Goetz (1840-1876) studied in Berlin with Bülow and other masters. His Pianoforte Concerto, opus 18, and the opera, *Der Widerspenstigen Zähmung,* were considered to be valuable additions to the musical literature of the time. An early Violin Concerto in B-flat major is little known.

38. Leipzig: F. Kistner, orchestra and pianoforte scores.

The orchestral accompaniment of the concerto is scored for

2 flutes	2 horns
2 oboes	tympani
2 clarinets	triangle
2 bassoons	strings

KARL REINECKE[39]

Reinecke's First Violin Concerto was written in 1857. Although there were immediate performances of it in Leipzig, the work was never printed. Concerto No. II in G minor, opus 141,[40] was composed in Leipzig in 1876 and published during the ensuing year. It was another of the voluminous series of concertos dedicated to Joachim, and was first performed by him in the Leipzig *Gewandhaus* (December 21, 1876).

The Allegro moderato of Concerto No. II, like the finale, reflects the influence of Mendelssohn. When Reinecke came to Leipzig in 1843, he cultivated the society of Mendelssohn, the result of which is attested in the emphasis on lyricism, clarity, consonance, and a traditional instrumentation. The orchestral exposition alludes to a prominent motive in the violoncello:

Theme I, a period of eleven measures, begins in measure 5; and the solo exposition commences (meas. 46) with a rhythmic modification of motive R and a statement of the main theme. A prolix

39. Reinecke (1824-1910) became widely known as a pianist, composer, conductor, and pedagogue. In 1860 he was appointed conductor of the Leipzig *Gewandhaus* orchestra, and professor of composition at the *Konservatorium*. He held the former position until the accession of Nikisch, in 1895. Reinecke's prolific compositions include piano pieces, chamber music, and the *Kinderlieder,* which are esteemed at the present time. Among his pupils were Bruch, Grieg, Hallén, and Chadwick.

40. Leipzig: Breitkopf und Härtel, orchestra score.

second theme appears in measure 98, and returns (meas. 297) in the reprise with a modified version given to the solo violin. A phrase from it occurs also in the clarinet part, while a canonical follower emerges in the horn part, two measures later. The prosaic cadenza was written out by the composer, and given its conventional position immediately preceding the coda. The harmonic structure of the movement is marked by conservative modulations and definitive cadences, such as those in G minor (meas. 86), B-flat major (164), and D major (194).

The Lento suffers from excessive repetitions and rhythmic monotony. We observe that the *divisi* violoncello part makes use of the *scordatura*, as the second violoncellos are directed to tune the G string down to F-sharp, and the C string to B. This is quite exceptional in the orchestration of the Romantic violin concerto.

The Finale (Moderato con grazia) features a theme with copious double-stops,

and has a tremolo accompaniment that recalls analogous figurations in Mendelssohn's Overture to *Fingal's Cave,* opus 26. An altered dominant thirteenth dissonance (meas. 13), preparing the entrance of the above theme, is particularly striking.

The accompaniment is scored for

2 flutes	3 trumpets
2 oboes	3 trombones
2 clarinets	tympani
2 horns	strings

Max Bruch[41]

A *Lexikon der Tonkunst* that was published a short time before Bruch composed his first violin concerto gave a surprisingly just evaluation of his merits and deficiencies as a composer: "Bruch certainly possesses an exceptional gift for composition; and when he acquires more polish (Geschlossenheit) and repose and learns to admit more naturalness and unaffectedness in his feelings and experiences, then the world may anticipate more significant achievements from him."[42]

His violin concertos were destined to become his most significant contributions to Romantic music. Like Goldmark and Tschaikowsky, Bruch was a virile creator who possessed an unexcelled "instinct" for the violin. To him the violin was essentially a *Gesangsinstrument,* admirably suited to a style that was characterized by fertility of invention, coloristic harmonies, solid contrapuntal technique, and free recitatives. His style revealed, moreover, an especial adeptness in the vocal forms.[43]

Although Bruch wrote three violin concertos, it is assumed that Concerto No. III, opus 58, will not come within the scope of this treatise because of its relatively late conception.[44] It reflected the influence of Brahms to an excessive degree, and was, generally, of

41. Bruch (1838-1920) evinced a remarkable talent for composition, even as a youth. After instruction under F. Hiller, Reinecke, and other pedagogues, Bruch began his extensive *Studienreisen.* Subsequently, he held various positions in Germany until his appointment, in 1891, as head of the master class in composition in the Berlin *Akademie.*

42. Bernsdorf (Hsg.), *Neues Universal-Lexikon der Tonkunst,* erster Nachtrag, 1865, p. 90.

43. Bruch's choral works, *Odysseus, Lied von der Glocke, Frithjof, Das Feuerkreuz,* and others, are of considerable interest.

44. Concerto No. III in D minor, opus 58, was composed during 1890-1891, and was dedicated to Joachim. The Allegro energico is in the conventional sonata form with a double exposition. Being neither free nor declamatory, it is quite unlike the opening movements of the composer's other concertos. Brahmsian idioms are prevalent in the second movement (Adagio), as we deduce from the oppositional rhythms (meas. 21). The Allegro molto has an attractive rhythmic vitality. A motive (meas. 5) recurs persistently throughout the movement.

inferior quality as compared to the composer's other concertos.

Concerto No. I in G minor, opus 26,[45] has been widely acclaimed as a Romantic *pièce de résistance*. First sketches of this work dated from 1857, but the composition was not completed until 1866-1867, when Bruch was in Coblenz and Sondershausen. The first performance took place in Coblenz on April 24, 1866, with the result that the composer deemed it necessary to make some drastic revisions in the composition. These were effected during the following summer. Bruch then dispatched the work to Joachim (to whom it was dedicated), and sought his criticism. It is evident, therefore, that the eminent violinist had a direct influence on the final version of the concerto, published in 1868.

A signal feature of the free and dramatic Vorspiel (Allegro moderato) is the elimination of both the orchestral exposition and the reprise. A soft tympani roll prepares the entrance of a prominent motive given to the flutes and clarinets:

The important recitatives of the solo violin part (meas. 6 and 10)

are complemented by reproductions of motive T in the orchestra. Theme I (meas. 16) is bold and virile:

45. Leipzig: C. F. W. Siegel, orchestra score.

Observe the *marcato* rhythmic motive in the accompaniment, as it becomes a vital cohesive factor in the movement.

Declamatory passages (meas. 31-40) in the solo violin part are intensified by the use of octaves and chords:

A typically strong and definitive cadence occurs in the dominant key (D minor) in measure 40. Theme II is a sensuous melody in the relative major key:

The accompaniment proceeds in contrary motion in the violin parts. Observe, also, the counterpoint in the violoncellos (meas. 52).

A compressed development section begins in measure 74. The rhythmic motive (X), previously mentioned, appears again; and dramatic violin arpeggios (meas. 98-106) rise to a climax. A powerful tutti (meas. 108) with extraneous passages is held together by the familiar rhythmic motive, now slightly altered. Motive U (meas. 118) reappears in the wood-winds and brasses in preparation for the return of Motive T (meas. 141) and modified versions of the recitatives (meas. 144, 148).[46] There is no formal reprise, however, as these recitatives "dissolve" into a brief cadenza for the solo violin. An orchestral transition, Allegro moderato (meas. 153), in E-flat major, leads directly into the second movement.

The Adagio movement, like the Air from the Concerto, opus 28, by Goldmark,[47] has a profound Romantic conception. The fine melodic texture, rich embellishment of the musical ideas, concentrative utilization of motives, and transcendence of metrical limitations by rhythmical patterns are among the expressive and technical aspects.

The design has the following ramifications: X (ritornello) — A — transition — B — A — X — A′ — B — coda (excerpts from B, X, and A). The first fifteen measures are designated as a ritornello:[48]

This melody recurs in measures 79-97 and 133-140. Section A (meas. 15-29) has a poignant theme in the principal key (E-flat):

46. Compare with measures 6 and 10.   47. See *infra*, p. 111.

48. This term is arbitrarily and conveniently used here to designate a few independent measures which function as an introduction and interlude. There is some affinity with its use in chanted poetry, where the ritornello appeared before, between, and after the various strophes.

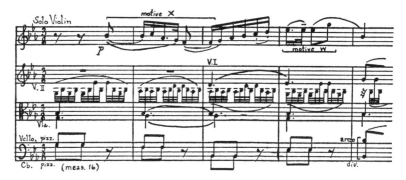

Its two motives, as well as the undulating accompaniment figures and the anacrusis, are significant in the movement. The transition (meas. 29-46) adapts the undulating figures and motive W to new phrases in the solo violin part. Section B (meas. 47-63) begins in the dominant key. A new theme in the bassoons, horns, violoncellos, and contrabasses is enhanced by variations in the solo violin:

The remaining sections of the movement may be listed briefly:

    A (meas. 63-78), with the main theme in the dominant key
    X (meas. 79-97), in the remote key of G-flat
    A' (meas. 97-118), with new elaborations
    B (meas. 119-129), abbreviated by one phrase
    Coda (meas. 129), with allusions to the previous sections

    The introduction to the Finale (Allegro energico) begins in the tonality of the previous movement (E-flat); but the tonic key

(G) is manifest in measure 11. A fundamental motive (meas. 3-4) in the first violins, violoncellos, and contrabasses is given a modified version in the presentation of the first theme. The incomparable *Schwung* of the movement is palpable in the character of the first theme:

This theme, in its complete form, is a phrase group (a, a′, b) with vital motives and figures. After vehement reproductions and elaborations of this material, there is an episode in sequential triplet patterns, derived from figure *h:*

We perceive a familiar conflict between rhythmic and metric patterns.

Measures 98-104 reveal an effective chromatic scale line in the violoncellos and contrabasses moving against the other voices in contrary motion. A pedal point in the first horn part is also conspicuous. Measures 104-162 are restated with some modifications in measures 213-281. In measure 104 we observe the beginning of an impassioned theme (flutes, oboes, clarinets, first violins, and violoncellos) in the dominant key (D):

A dramatic reproduction of it is given to the solo violin, on the G string (meas. 116-132). Subsequently (meas. 136-145), the solo violin variates another part of this theme:

The appearance of motive Y in the orchestra against new triplet figurations in the solo part (meas. 146) marks the beginning of a codetta section. This later recurs (meas. 253) transposed to the tonic key.

A rather fragmentary and modulatory section (meas. 162-213) begins with a partial restatement of theme I in the dominant key. This is followed by a partial restatement of the theme in the solo violin part (meas. 181-188) in the tonic key. Manipulations of this material involve persistent reiterations of motive Z and figures *h* and *m*.

It will be recalled that measures 213-281 constitute a reproduction of measures 104-162; however, theme II is transposed to the tonic key and now sets forth a vigorous canon,

the second phrase of which is taken up by the solo violin (meas. 221) and emulated, one measure later, by the canonical follower in the violoncellos and first bassoon.

A striking cadence evasion and powerful climax (meas. 281) inaugurate the coda—again with allusions to theme I. The speed is accelerated as extraneous material with syncopations is introduced (meas. 297), and motive K and figure *h* are regnant in the orchestra. The cadence section (Presto) exploits figure *m* in the solo violin part, intensifying the close of a remarkably cohesive movement.

Bruch's Concerto No. II in D minor, opus 44,[49] was composed in Bonn in 1877. Its première took place in London on November 4 of that year, with the Spanish violinist, Sarasate (to whom the work was dedicated), as soloist. With its importation of the *principe cyclique,* its dramatic pathos, irregular phraseology, rhythmic vitality, and consummate adaptability to the violin, this work has a worthy and dignified place in Romantic music.

The first movement (Adagio, ma non troppo) has an eloquent theme,

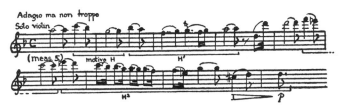

that moves sequentially against the supporting harmony. The principal motive is of fundamental importance because of its recurrence in the second movement. Thus it provides a cyclical link in the form of the whole. A transition divulges a heavily accented ("heroic") rhythm:

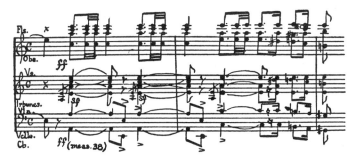

Following a pronouncement of the second theme in the relative

49. Berlin: Simrock, orchestra score.

major key (meas. 52), there is a terse development section that
begins with a dolorous phrase in the low registers:

This reappears in the coda (meas. 166), in the tonic major key.
A brief solo cadenza (meas. 109-115) leads into a conventional
reprise (meas. 116); and there is an impressive *Ausklang* as the
movement concludes.

The Recitative (Allegro moderato) has a rhapsodical character.
The introductory section embraces an orchestral tutti and a recitative in the solo violin. The latter begins with a "call" motive,

that recurs in the concluding four measures of the movement,
and also in the Finale (meas. 14 *et al.*), thus serving as a transitional link between the two movements. Motive H, from theme I
of the first movement,[50] is then introduced and promptly "dis-
solved" into a rapid arpeggio:

Similar manifestations of the *principe cyclique* are evident in the
works of Berlioz, Wagner, Franck, Raff, Dvořák, and other
Romanticists. A vigorous theme (meas. 23) in the contrasting
section (Allegro) appears in the key of G minor, and later returns
in C minor.

The redundant Finale (Allegro molto) has an interesting and
somewhat irregular sonata form. It begins with a long transitional section (151 measures), in which there is further evidence

50. See *supra*, p. 101.

of the *principe cyclique* as the familiar "call" motive from the second movement reappears, expanded into a transitional theme. It is first stated in the sub-mediant major key (B-flat), and is given a new metrical pattern:

Motive T is substantially manipulated during the course of the movement. The phrases quoted above could be more appropriately set in a flexible metrical scheme with the time signatures:

9-8, meas. 14	9-8, meas. 27
6-8, meas. 17	6-8, meas. 30
9-8, meas. 19	9-8, meas. 34
6-8, meas. 25	12-8, meas. 37

The main theme (meas. 169) appears in the tonic major key:

The logical meter is 6-8.

Other formal details in the movement include:

1. Second theme (meas. 296), a scale line melody in F major
2. Codetta (meas. 375), in the tonic minor key
3. Development (meas. 411), commencing in F major with the main theme given to the flutes and violins
4. Reprise (meas. 581), containing restatements of both principal themes in the tonic major key
5. Coda (meas. 747), embracing another statement of the main theme, and motive T in the orchestra against virtuosic passages in the solo violin part.

Idiomatic passages in this long movement include the chromatic octaves in measures 403-406, and the figurations from the codetta cited in the following example:

We might also mention other specific features, such as the emphasis on mediant key relationships, facile modulations, numerous suspensions, and frequent use of anacrusis and syncopation.

The orchestral accompaniment of this concerto requires:

2 flutes	4 horns
2 oboes	2 trumpets
2 clarinets	3 trombones
2 bassoons	tympani
strings	

Excepting the trombones, the same orchestra is employed for the Concerto in G minor, opus 26. A specific fault of the orchestration in both works is the excessive use of the bowed tremolo. On the other hand, the accompaniment is favored with considerable thematic participation, and fuses remarkably well with the solo violin part. In this and other respects, both of these concertos may be regarded as meritorious precursors of the Brahms Concerto, opus 77.

FERDINAND HILLER[51]

This composer was ". . . not free from obvious eclecticism; moreover, in the large forms, he was unable to hold one's interest

51. Like his friend Mendelssohn, Hiller (1811-1885) was the scion of wealthy parents, and the recipient of unusual educational opportunities. He met Beethoven in Vienna, in 1827, and for the next seven years resided in Paris, where he consorted with Cherubini, Rossini, Chopin, Berlioz, Meyerbeer, and Liszt. He was a versatile musician, being a pianist, conductor, composer, pedagogue, and author.

for any length of time."[52] The opinion is substantiated in the prolix Concerto in A major, opus 152.[53] The Allegro grazioso has, however, an alluring Mozartian theme:

This theme, of irregular phrase length, recurs in the development (dominant key, meas. 203; and C major, meas. 279) and in the reprise (meas. 312). A worthy cadenza by Joachim (to whom the concerto was dedicated) precedes the coda. The melodic idioms, embellishments, and accompaniment of the Andante espressivo reveal the composer's affinity with Spohr. The finale, Allegro con fuoco, suffers from an effete accompaniment and excessive melodic repetitions.

LEOPOLD DAMROSCH[54]

The holograph score of Damrosch's Concerto in F-sharp minor bears the inscription: "Zweites Concert für die Violine mit Begleitung des Orchesters componiert von Leopold Damrosch.

52. Batka and Nagel, *Allgemeine Geschichte der Musik,* Vol. III, p. 129.

53. Mainz: B. Schott Söhne, pianoforte score.

54. Leopold Damrosch (1832-1885) was graduated from the University of Berlin in 1854 with an M.D. degree. Despite the opposition of his parents, he devoted himself to a musical career. In 1857 he was appointed violinist to the Court of Weimar. There he made the acquaintance of Liszt, Bülow, Wagner, Tausig, Raff, Cornelius, and other eminent musicians. In 1871 Damrosch accepted the appointment as conductor of a choral society in New York. Later, he founded the New York Oratorio Society and the New York Symphony Society. His compositions include three violin concertos, in G major, F-sharp minor, and D minor, respectively. The latter work was dedicated to Joachim, and the orchestral score was published by Bote and Bock in 1878. A score is available at the Library of Congress.

Partitur. New York. August 1877."[55] It represents, we are informed, a rather extensive revision of an earlier work.[56]

The first theme of the Allegro ma non troppo, appassionata,
is enunciated by the solo violin, in measure 5. A facile harmoniza-
tion of it marks the inception of the development. Note especially
the concluding chords of the example:

The canon

and a similar example from the finale (meas. 139-144) are depar-
tures from the homophonic texture of the concerto. A repetition
of the second theme by the flute and clarinet reveals an arabesque
figuration in the solo violin part:

55. This holograph was graciously lent to the author by Dr. Walter Damrosch.
56. The movements of this earlier version were: (1) Allegro ma non troppo,
appassionata, (2) Trauergesang, adagio con duolo, (3) Finale, molto vivace.

We have the beginning of the reprise with the return of this theme in the tonic major key (meas. 239). There is no restatement of theme I; and no formal cadenza appears in this or the other movements.

An interesting study is offered in the comparison of parts 1 and 3 of the Lento. Part 3 (meas. 52) is a modified presentation of the first part.

The accompaniment of the Quasi presto, molto con fuoco, is similar to that employed in the finale of Joachim's *Hungarian* Concerto, opus 11. The design is as follows:

> Introduction
> Section A (meas. 9)
> Section B (meas. 88)
> Miniature development (meas. 139)
> Section A (meas. 168)
> Section B (meas. 247)
> Coda

The first theme contains propulsive leaps

over chordal repetitions and a pedal bass in the accompaniment. The harmonic minor scale is frequently utilized.

The orchestral accompaniment requires:

2 flutes	2 horns
2 oboes	2 trumpets
2 clarinets	tympani
2 bassoons	strings

There is, perhaps, an excessive predominance of the solo violin part, and too little activity in the brass instrument parts.

Karl Goldmark[57]

Goldmark, like his contemporaries, Brahms and Bruch, commanded an exceedingly skillful technique of composition. A rich imagination, sensuous melos, kaleidoscopic harmony, solid contrapuntal technique, and rhythmic vitality distinguish the Violin Concerto in A minor, opus 28.[58]

In the Allegro moderato a resolute tutti of twenty-one measures features a significant motive with an iambic rhythm:

Chromatic progressions assume a preferential role in the concerto, as shown in the following example:

The poignant main theme is first enunciated by the solo violin:

A modulation to the relative major key (C) is manifest in meas-

57. Goldmark (1830-1915) was born in Keszthely, Hungary. His musical education at the Vienna *Konservatorium* was curtailed by the Revolution of 1848. His Concerto, opus 28, was first performed in Vienna in 1878; and its first American performance took place in Boston on December 6, 1890, with Franz Kneisel as soloist, and A. Nikisch, the conductor. In addition to this work, Goldmark composed another violin concerto (without an opus number).

58. Hamburg: Pohle, orchestra score.

ures 22-23. After a cadence in A minor (meas. 65-66) and the return of motive H, the solo violin unfolds variations over sequential two-measure phrases in the orchestra with a new version of motive H:

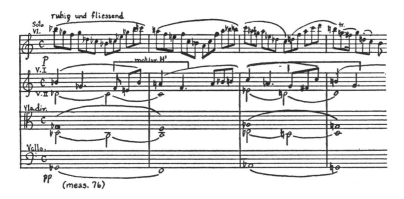

The harmony in this section is characterized by fleeting, transient modulations. The mood of the second theme is *innig* and religious:

The key is G major. Observe the contrary motion in the viola part and the deliberate tremolos in the second violins. As the theme

ascends into the upper registers, it is doubled by the clarinet
(meas. 120). A lyrical section, featuring motive H², brings the
exposition to a close in the dominant major key (E):

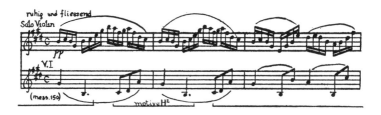

The development begins with a fugato (meas. 203) in which
the solo instrument has no part. The subject

is generated from motive H. The answer enters in the second
violins; the next presentation of the subject enters in the first
violins; and the fourth voice (violoncellos and contrabasses) returns the subject instead of the answer. A similar fugal exposition
is utilized in the finale.[59] Not since the time of Bach and his
Baroque contemporaries have we found this contrapuntal form
applied to the violin concerto. Even then, we recall that the concerto type of that day was intrinsically different from the solo
concerto of the Romantic period.

The abbreviated recapitulation (meas. 264) is preceded by a
brief cadenza (Tempo, poco sostenuto), which serves as a transition from the tutti. A series of difficult violin passages over motive
H marks the beginning of a new episode (meas. 374). A powerful
tutti (meas. 443), in which motive H again predominates, closes
the movement.

59. See *infra*, p. 112.

The Air (Andante) may be regarded as one of the most august and inspired movements in the Romantic violin literature. The form is ternary: introduction — A — B — A — coda. The introduction, modulating from F major through E minor to G major, leads to an expressive theme in the last key:

The contrasting section (Poco animato) is distinguished for its shifting harmonies and transient key changes. A pulsating transitional passage (meas. 66) over a dominant pedal-point

rises to a grandiose climax (meas. 73). In measure 88 the theme returns, but with its antecedent phrase consigned to the G string of the solo violin. A coda of ten measures gives a tranquil *Ausklang.*

For the concluding movement Goldmark departs from the conventional tradition by utilizing the sonata form. After a brief Moderato introduction, a jaunty Polacca theme, somewhat reminiscent of Rode and Spohr, inaugurates the movement proper (Allegretto):

Note the close relationship of motives R and H[60] and the vital syncopations. An impassioned second theme (G major) ascends to the high registers:

The exposition closes in the favored key of G major (meas. 128), and is linked with the development by means of a transitional episode.[61] As in the first movement, the development (meas. 148) commences with a fugal exposition in the strings, the subject of which

60. See *supra*, p. 108.

61. A rather similar transition was employed for the same purpose in the first movement (meas. 194-202).

is derived from theme I. Motive R^1 is subsequently utilized as a counterpoint to a new but relatively unimportant melody in D major (meas. 170).

Goldmark, like Mendelssohn, Joachim, and Bruch, wrote out his own cadenza. It is ninety-six measures in length, and features thematic excerpts together with intricate double-stopping and *ricochet* bowing styles. A rather unusual example of the latter is found at the point where the orchestra re-enters:

The return of themes I and II, in A minor and A major, respectively, is followed by a coda (Poco più mosso) with brilliant passages in the solo part.

The scoring of the concerto includes:

2 flutes	4 horns
2 oboes	2 trumpets
2 clarinets	3 trombones
2 bassoons	tympani
strings	

It represents a definite advancement in orchestral technique, not only because of the augmented size of the accompanying groups, but also because the orchestra functions in the role of a symphonic collaborator.

ALBERT HERMANN DIETRICH[62]

Dietrich was a virile writer and a good melodist; but like some other minor composers of this epoch, he seemed to lack the capacity to create a style which was truly his own.

The Allegro of the Concerto in D minor, opus 30,[63] contains

62. Dietrich (1829-1908) attended the University of Leipzig where he had musical instruction under Rietz, Hauptmann, and Moscheles. He was also a pupil of Schumann and a close friend of Brahms.
63. Hamburg: Pohle, pianoforte score.

a second theme that has been termed "besonders schön, satt und dunkel":

The motives indicated are prominent in the subsequent manipulations. The violin cadenza, accompanied, was written out by the composer. The main theme of the Adagio expressivo

possesses an egregious similarity to the clarinet theme in Beethoven's Overture to *Leonore* No. III (meas. 9-11), and also to the first theme of the Allegro affettuoso (meas. 4-7) of the Schumann Piano Concerto, opus 54. The finale, Allegro molto vivace, is archaic and sentimental.

FRIEDRICH GERNSHEIM [64]

"A skillful composer, adept in all forms and capable of varied expression, and yet without the convincing power of inner necessity ..." [65] is Riemann's evaluation of this Romanticist. Gernsheim's compositions include two violin concertos. The Violin Concerto in D major, opus 42,[66] was composed in Rotterdam between July

64. Gernsheim (1839-1916) spent most of his student years in Leipzig and Paris. In later years he held various positions in Cologne, Rotterdam, and Berlin.
65. Riemann, *Geschichte der Musik seit Beethoven*, p. 569.
66. Leipzig and Winterthur: J. Rieter-Biedermann, orchestra score.

and October, 1879,[67] a relatively short time after the first performance of the Brahms Concerto, opus 77.[68] The terse themes,
anacrusis, oppositional rhythms, and technique of orchestration
betray Gernsheim as an epigone of Brahms.

A specimen of the oppositional rhythms is taken from the
Allegro non troppo of the Concerto in D, opus 42:

This is definitely Brahmsian. Massive figures in contrary motion
(cf. meas. 51 *et al.*) are also reminiscent of Brahms. The form of
this movement is irregular. The return of the first theme takes
place in the coda; and the cadenza marks the beginning of the
development.

The Andante affettuoso, in the mediant key (F-sharp minor),
begins with an expressive cantilena:

A ternary form is used.

The Allegro energico e con brio has three themes, in the keys
of D major, F-sharp minor, and A major, respectively. These
themes return, and a coda (L'istesso tempo) that recalls Brahms
concludes the movement. Another example of the Brahmsian
influence is seen in the following excerpt:

67. Müller-Reuter, *Lexikon der deutschen Konzertliteratur,* Vol. I, pp. 579-580.
68. See *infra,* p. 128.

The scoring of the accompaniment requires:

2 flutes	4 horns
2 oboes	2 trumpets
2 clarinets	tympani
2 bassoons	strings

IGNAZ BRÜLL[69]

With his operas and instrumental works Brüll achieved a reputation as a worthy and routined composer. Among the instrumental works was a Violin Concerto, opus 41.[70]

The Allegro con brio of this concerto is devoid of contrapuntal textures and is generally lacking in solid content. The second theme (meas. 76) appears to be in E minor, with a prominent lowered seventh degree. A virtuosic cadenza near the close of the movement recalls some of the technical idioms of Lipinski. The principal melody of the Molto moderato has prolix repetitions that divulge one of the composer's most serious weaknesses. On the other hand, the concluding Allegro is an interesting movement because of its exotic modal harmonies and individualistic passage types. The Aeolian mode is apparent in the first phrase of the second theme:

69. Brüll (1846-1907) was born in Prossnitz, Moravia. He studied in Vienna and first made his reputation there as a pianist and composer. His opera, *Das goldene Kreuz,* was performed in various European capitals and in America. Brüll's intimate friends included Goldmark, Mahler, Brahms, Rubinstein, Joachim, and Sarasate.   70. Vienna: J. Gutmann (422).

This archaic modal quality constitutes a striking innovation in the Romantic violin concerto. We recall, however, that it is typical of plain song, numerous folk expressions, and Impressionistic idioms.

The orchestral accompaniment embraces:

2 flutes	3 horns
2 oboes	2 trumpets
2 clarinets	tympani
2 bassoons	strings

Philippe Barthélemy Rüfer[71]

Some of the violin idioms of this writer's Concerto in D minor, opus 33,[72] are exceedingly difficult. Excerpts from the first movement are quoted:

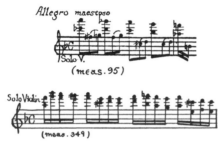

The first theme is not well-defined; and there is no cadenza in any of the movements. Various pedal effects are prominent; for example, those on *c* (meas. 98-105) and on the dominant (meas. 321-328). There are embellished pedals in the Adagio (meas. 37-41 and 74-81; horn parts). This slow movement also betrays the influence of Bruch, as we may infer from the embellishments in the solo part. The difficult, concluding Allegro is reminiscent of the Rondo (Allegro) in Beethoven's Violin Concerto, opus 61. Observe, especially, the broken octave passages.

71. Rüfer (1844-1919) was born in Liége, Belgium. He was the son of a German organist, and spent most of his musical career in Germany.
72. Leipzig: Peters, orchestra score.

The accompaniment of the concerto is scored for

2 flutes	2 horns
2 oboes	2 trumpets
2 clarinets	tympani
2 bassoons	strings

Hans Sitt[73]

As a creator, Sitt was lacking in originality; but his sound knowledge of violin technicalities has made his three violin concertos quite useful for purposes of study. We shall interest ourselves specifically in his Concerto in A minor, opus 21.[74] The design of the Allegro moderato is rather similar to that of the first movement in Wieniawski's Concerto, opus 22. An incomplete sonata form is employed, for no reprise succeeds the development section. There are evidences of the *principe cyclique;* for the solo violin enters (meas. 17) with improvisatory phrases that return in the Moderato section of the finale. Compare, for example, measures 5-14 of the latter with measures 17-26 of the first movement. Motive H, from the Mendelssohnian first theme,

reasserts itself frequently in the concluding movement. The development leads into a transition, the conclusion of which (meas. 216-219) sets forth an augmentation of a motive from the principal melody of the second movement.

The Andante tranquillo (B-flat major) proceeds without pause, as it is connected to the previous movement by means of an F-seventh chord. The principal melody

---

73. Sitt (1850-1922) enjoyed a considerable reputation as a pedagogue at the Leipzig *Konservatorium.* He was also for some time the violist in the Brodsky Quartet.   74. Leipzig: Leuckart, pianoforte score.

is given a new metrical version in the finale:

The concluding five measures (of the second movement) are similar to the close of the Andante in Mendelssohn's Concerto, opus 64. There is formal clarity, but the compositional technique is otherwise superficial.

The finale suffers from a lack of originality. The movement begins with a Moderato (14 measures) to which we have already referred. The statement of the principal theme (meas. 21) contains motive H from the first movement:

RICHARD STRAUSS[75]

The Concerto for Violin and Orchestra in D minor, opus 8,[76] was composed in 1883, when Strauss was but nineteen years of age. It is conservative "absolute" music that cannot be regarded on the

75. Strauss was born in Munich in 1864. He was the son of an excellent hornist—a circumstance that was reflected in the conception of a Horn Concerto, opus 11. He attended the University of Munich (1882-1883), and later (1885) succeeded von Bülow as conductor of the Meiningen Orchestra. It was also about this time that he made the acquaintance of Alexander von Ritter. A brief period of travel in Italy led to the composition of a series of dynamic tone-poems. International recognition followed. After appointments as *Hofkapellmeister* in Munich and Berlin, Strauss was made *Generalmusikdirektor* in the latter city (1908). In more recent years he has resided in Vienna and Garmisch-Partenkirchen.

76. Leipzig: J. Aibl, orchestra score.

same niveau with the composer's *Tod und Verklärung, Till Eulenspiegel, Don Quixote, Salome,* and *Elektra.*

The orchestral introduction of the opening Allegro features an important motive:

This motive becomes the generator of a theme (in the development section) cited by Engel[77] as an example of the Strauss cantilena (meas. 222). Other analytical traits of the movement are enumerated briefly:

1. The solo exposition commences (meas. 27) with double-stop passages which begin the recapitulation and also provide the impetus for brief cadenzas (meas. 195-199, 206-210) in the development.

2. Theme I (meas. 38-61) comprises three irregular phrases (6+6+12 measures).

3. Theme II (meas. 98-116) is a redundant phrase in the relative major key (F).

4. The development (meas. 168) begins in F major. A new theme (meas. 222), already referred to, is accompanied by a cognate melody in the first bassoon part (meas. 224).

5. The orthodox recapitulation (meas. 248) embraces a literal repetition of theme I and a transposition of theme II to the parallel major key (D). The coda begins in measure 389.

The contrasting middle section of the second movement (Lento) offers an example of mild polyphonic texture:

77. Engel, *Das Instrumentalkonzert* (Führer durch den Konzertsaal, begonnen von H. Kretzschmar. *Die Orchestermusik,* Vol. III), p. 499. The fifth measure of the example is incorrectly quoted by Engel.

The difficult Rondo (Presto) is exceedingly long. A tarantella rhythm characterizes the main theme:

Other formal sections include:

Section B (meas. 75), cantabile second theme

Section C (meas. 139) in the dominant key (A major), new theme (meas. 141) and subsequent allusions to main theme

Section A (meas. 311)

Section D (meas. 375), new theme in sub-dominant key

Section A (meas. 437) with modifications

Section B (meas. 525)

Section C (meas. 589) in the tonic key

Andante (meas. 701), a transitional episode with a melodic figure from theme II of the first movement, leading directly into the coda (meas. 707), designated Prestissimo

The accompaniment is scored for

2 flutes	4 horns
2 oboes	2 trumpets
2 clarinets	tympani
2 bassoons	strings

The subservient function of the orchestra offers a marked contrast with the virtuosic and glittering instrumentation in a work such as the composer's *Don Quixote*.

SUMMARY

In the diverse violin concertos of this chapter we have observed a significant advancement as compared, for example, to the work of the Romanticists discussed in Chapter III. Since those earlier composers remained primarily violin virtuosi, they naturally formulated conceptions in terms of pyrotechnical effects. The later Romanticists, however, interested themselves essentially in the musical and esthetic content of the concerto.

Some of these composers were hampered in their achievements because of the fact that they possessed little more than a theoretical acquaintance with the violin. Thus Schumann, Raff, Goetz, Gernsheim, Brüll, and Rüfer conceived idioms that were pianistic and not always effective for the violin.

Raff was subject to the dominant influence of the Liszt circle, and used a programmatic connotation for his Concerto, opus 206. Like him, Joachim was swayed by the creed of the Liszt group, although he soon altered his course to the standard of "absolute" music.

Joachim, as a virtuoso, had a profound influence on his contemporaries, for many of them either wrote their concertos directly for him, or were inspired by him. In his own compositions he was an innovator, being among the first Romanticists to adapt the folk tune to the violin concerto. In this use of folk tunes he was preceded by Spohr and Maurer, and was followed by Tschaikowsky, Dvořák, and others.

Both Joachim and Schumann were vitally interested in stimulating appreciation of the Classical masters. We are hardly surprised, therefore, that a contemporary, Joseph Hellmesberger, undertook the completion of an early concerto fragment by Beethoven.

Formal innovations which are manifest in the works of this chapter may be listed briefly:

1. Concerto in one movement (Goetz, Concerto, opus 22). The various sections make up a large ternary design with a coda.

2. Adaptation of the *principe cyclique* to the violin concerto (Bruch, Concerto, opus 44). This recalls experiments in other genres by Berlioz, Wagner, Franck, Tschaikowsky, and Dvořák.

3. Use of the sonata form in the finale (Raff, Bruch, Goldmark).

4. Irregular designs (Bruch).

5. Elimination of the orchestral exposition (Goetz, Bruch).

6. Elimination of the reprise (Bruch, first movement of Concerto, opus 26).

7. Elimination of the violin cadenza (Schumann, Raff, Bruch, Damrosch, Rüfer).

8. Cadenza written out by the composer (Joachim, Reinecke, Goldmark, Goetz, Dietrich, Gernsheim).

Since the publication of the Mendelssohn Concerto, opus 64, it became a more common procedure for the Romanticists to utilize small motives as basic formal units. The consignment of these motives and frequent thematic exchanges to the orchestra, in addition to the fact that the orchestra was gradually augmented in dimensions, leads us to assume there were essential contributions to the progress of instrumentation.

Harmonic combinations were frequently employed as a medium for color. Thus we have the archaic quality of the ecclesiastical modes as used by Brüll, and the opulent chromatic and enharmonic modulations of Goldmark. New concepts of dissonance were also apparent.

The technique of counterpoint became increasingly significant with writers such as Goldmark and Bruch. It is worthy of repetition that the former inserted fugal expositions in both the first and last movements of his Concerto, opus 28.

Rhythmic structures were diverse. The "autocracy" of the bar line was less dominant, as revealed in the anacrustic rhythms and syncopations of Bruch, Goetz, Goldmark, and Gernsheim. Bruch, in his Concerto, opus 26, used a basic rhythmic motive as a cohesive factor in the first movement.

The emotional content was more varied and profound. The ingenuousness of the folk tunes, the sensuous warmth of Goldmark's expressions, the dramatic pathos of Bruch, and a regard for the psychological effect of the climax were aspects of this development.

In general, we may assume that Goldmark's enharmony and

chromaticism remind us of Spohr; Bruch's declamatory style and free recitatives also revert to Spohr; Brüll's employment of the old modes reveals an affinity with the technique of the Impressionists; and, finally, Raff, Reinecke, Hiller, Damrosch, Dietrich, Gernsheim, Rüfer, Sitt, and even Strauss may be regarded as eclectic and conventional writers who adhered to conservative traditions and standards of the time.

JOHANNES BRAHMS[1]

O N MARCH 11, 1848, Brahms heard Joachim play the Beethoven Violin Concerto in Hamburg. The impression which the work and the performer made on Johannes as he listened that evening was profound. A subsequent meeting with Joachim in Göttingen[2] was indeed a fortunate circumstance; for in him Brahms found affectionate understanding, inspiration, and unselfish devotion to high and lofty ideals. It was through Joachim, moreover, that Brahms made the acquaintance of Schumann. The latter was then in Düsseldorf, and soon took it upon himself to inform the musical world about the new genius.[3]

A short time later (December 17, 1853), Brahms appeared in a

1. Brahms was born in Hamburg on May 7, 1833. He received an adequate training in music theory from Eduard Marxsen. A source of inspiration to him during his student days was the opportunity to hear eminent artists such as Robert and Clara Schumann, David, Joachim, Jenny Lind, Henrietta Sontag, and others. When Brahms was twenty-nine years of age, he moved to Vienna, where he resided until his death in 1897.

2. "Asked to give a demonstration of his art, Brahms sat down to the piano and played his E-flat minor Scherzo and some movements from his C major Sonata. Joachim was astonished at the performer and even more at what he played. There was no more doubt in the mind of the enchanted listener. He had met an artist of equal rank, a towering genius by God's grace."—M. Kalbeck, *Johannes Brahms,* Vol. I, pp. 74-75.

3. Schumann, "Neue Bahnen," in the *Neue Zeitschrift für Musik* (October 28, 1853), Vol. XXXIX, pp. 185-186.

concert in Leipzig in which he played some of his own piano compositions. The reactions to his performance are reflected in the following quotation, taken from a publication of that time: "Immediately there developed two factions: the enthusiasts (Exaltados) and the moderates (Moderados). The former, comprising Neo-Romanticists, were delighted with the bold originality and significance of Brahms' talent. . . . The moderates, to be sure, found talent and much boldness, but also excessive crudity, awkwardness, and immaturity." They considered ". . . this audacity rather as a presumption . . ., which defies the laws of beauty and is guilty of irregularities without having recognized and understood the laws and rules. . . ."[4] This latter judgment seems quite strange and antithetical to our present opinion of Brahms; for we regard him as a rigorous apostle of the "laws" of beauty. Like the Classical masters, he believed that formal restriction existed only for him who was not the master of it. "Show me any work of Beethoven," he once said, "where the form is not strictly observed. . . ."[5]

In the polyphonic style Brahms' idol was J. S. Bach.[6] He studied Bach's compositions indefatigably and, as a result, became a master of contrapuntal textures and forms. Other well-defined traits in his work are represented by the individualistic and opulent harmonies with harsh but logical dissonances, irregular phraseology, concentrative use of thematic material, and flexible rhythmic concepts that involve anacrusis and syncopation. There is no work in which Brahms reveals these stylistic features more conspicuously than in his Concerto for Violin and Orchestra in D major, opus

4. Bernsdorf (Hsg.), *Neues Universal-Lexikon der Tonkunst, 1856,* Vol. I, p. 447.
5. Kalbeck, *Johannes Brahms,* Vol. II, p. 181.
6. Kalbeck related an amusing incident that occurred during the summer of 1889. One evening Joachim had finished playing a solo sonata by Bach, after which he and Brahms decided to perform the latter's Sonata in G, opus 78. When Brahms struck some wrong chords, he became enraged and arose from the piano. The music of Bach was still sounding in his ears, and his own composition, by comparison, seemed "banal."—*Ibid.,* Vol. IV, p. 170.

77.[7] It is a masculine structure, which towers aloft like a Gothic cathedral with its pinnacles, spires, pointed arches, and rich carvings.[8]

The origin of this violin concerto is perhaps more clearly known to us than that of any other composition by Brahms. The work was begun during the summer of 1878 while the composer was enjoying a holiday on Lake Wörther, in Pörtschach, Carinthia. On August 22 Brahms sent the violin part to Joachim and sought the latter's criticism: "Naturally I wish to ask you to correct it. I thought you ought to have no excuse . . . neither respect for its being too good music nor the pretext that the score would not merit the effort. Now I shall be satisfied if you say a word and perhaps write in several: difficult, awkward, impossible, etc. The composition has four movements. I wrote the beginning of the last one so that the awkward figures would be ruled out immediately."[9]

Joachim, after perusing the manuscript, was favorably impressed, and wrote: "I have looked through what you sent me, and you will find here and there a notation and correction . . . to be sure, one cannot enjoy it without a score. I can make out the most of it; and some things appear to be quite violinistic . . . but whether or not the work can be played with comfort in a warm concert hall is difficult for me to ascertain until I have heard it as a whole."[10]

Brahms informed the eminent violinist that he wished to send the orchestra score to him. Then he declared: "The middle movements have been discarded . . . of course they were the best! Now I am writing a feeble Adagio."[11] It is possible that the Scherzo may have found its rightful place as the Allegro appassionato of Brahms' Pianoforte Concerto, opus 83.

7. Orchestra scores, Simrock and Eulenberg.
8. W. Niemann, *Brahms,* pp. 275-276 (after Riemann).
9. A. Moser (Hsg.), *Johannes Brahms im Briefwechsel mit Joseph Joachim,* Vol. II, pp. 126-127.   10. *Ibid.,* p. 127, a letter dated August 24, 1878.
11. *Ibid.,* p. 133.

Joachim later wrote Brahms that he was seriously intent upon the composition of a cadenza. He studied the manuscript assiduously and suggested various *ossias,* as well as bowings and fingerings for the solo part. He also reminded Brahms of the extraordinary difficulties of the work.

The concerto was dedicated to Joachim, and was performed for the first time in a *Gewandhaus* concert in Leipzig on New Year's Day, 1879, with Joachim as the soloist and Brahms as conductor. The auditors listened with "respect," but were moved to no enthusiasm.[12] Hanslick regarded the work as a composition of masterful form and assimilation, but ". . . of a rather desiccated invention, and, as it were, with the half-stretched sails of an ebbing imagination."[13]

Neither Brahms nor Joachim was dismayed. Their correspondence about the work continued. Brahms insisted, ". . . you are not bold and severe enough. Only through many suggestions and alterations will you be able to impress me!"[14] Then, in a subsequent communication, he reiterated his desire for a detailed and frank criticism: "But I am very curious to learn how frequently and energetically your handwriting is revealed in the orchestra score and solo part; whether I shall be 'convinced,' or whether I must ask someone else . . . which I do not wish to do. In brief, is the piece sufficiently good and practicable to warrant its publication?"[15]

In the meantime Joachim had performed the concerto in Budapest, Vienna, and London.[16] Despite the fact that it was published by Simrock during the same year (1879), few musicians

12. Kalbeck, *Johannes Brahms,* Vol. III, pp. 211-212.

13. E. Hanslick, *Concerte, Componisten und Virtuosen der letzten fünfzehn Jahre: 1870-1885,* p. 268.

14. Moser (Hsg.), *Johannes Brahms im Briefwechsel mit Joseph Joachim,* Vol. II, p. 139.   15. *Ibid.,* p. 142.

16. Joachim played the concerto in Budapest one week after the première in Leipzig. The Vienna performance took place on January 14, and the first performance in London occurred on February 22, 1879.

manifested any real interest in it. The minority, however, included eminent violinists such as De Ahna, Halir, Heermann, Brodsky, and Soldat, who eventually became widely known for their authoritative renditions of the difficult work.

ANALYSIS

The artistic creed of Brahms is revealed in the serious and inexorable quality of the first movement, Allegro non troppo. The broad orchestral exposition is eighty-nine measures long. The main theme is announced at the beginning by the bassoons, violas, and violoncellos, reinforced in the fourth measure by two horns:

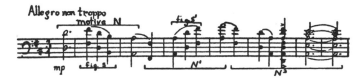

This ingenuous theme, constructed almost entirely from the tonic chord, recalled to Hanslick the opening theme of Beethoven's *Eroica* Symphony. Motives N, N^1, and N^2 are used in a concentrative manner during the course of the movement. The continuation of the theme

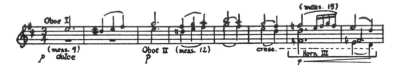

merits some comment, because Joachim complained that he "lost" the melody in the crescendo of the strings. He suggested, accordingly, that Brahms have the E horns (III and IV) play along with the solo oboe after the first two or three measures.[17] This caused Brahms to add these horns for the crescendo in measures 15-16, but with only the third horn doubling the melodic line.

17. Moser (Hsg.), *Johannes Brahms im Briefwechsel mit Joseph Joachim*, Vol. II, p. 151. The letter was written from Berlin on May 26, 1879.

A sudden *fp* ushers in a transparent phrase that we shall designate theme II A:

This phrase, which is but one of two subordinate themes in the movement, is extended so that it encompasses twenty-four measures. It modulates from the dominant minor key[18] to the tonic major key, and then passes through a series of chromatic transitions. Motive R is important, since it is manipulated:

Observe the familiar conflict of rhythm and meter. The closing theme, in a jagged iambic rhythm, appears in the tonic minor key:

and recurs in the solo exposition in the dominant minor key (meas. 247).

18. The shift to this minor key (meas. 42) from the parallel major key (A) discloses a typical Brahmsian harmonic trait. This logical parallelism is also conspicuous in the following:

(meas.   1) Orchestral exposition begins in D major.
(meas. 90) Solo exposition begins in D minor.
(meas. 206) Theme II B begins in A major.
(meas. 246) Closing theme begins in A minor.
(meas. 288) Section II of the development begins in C major.
(meas. 304) Section III of the development begins in C minor.

The entrance of the solo violin (meas. 90), with an expansion of motive N, is spectacular and dramatic:

This is followed by a modified repetition (meas. 95-98). Succeeding passages are awkward and unviolinistic:[19]

A tonic six-four chord is reached (meas. 120) with the ingenious overlapping of motive N in the strings against an embellished version of it in the solo part:

This overlapping technique is fundamental with Brahms.

The first appearance of the main theme in the solo exposition occurs in measure 136:

19. They are all the more difficult because of the necessity for playing them with the lower half of the bow.

Its continuation in the first violins (meas. 152) is ornamented by improvisatory but suggestive figurations in the solo violin. Theme II A (meas. 178) is announced by the first flute and is suffused by a variation in the solo violin part. A modulation is made to the dominant key before the familiar extensions commence with their evasive and shifting harmonies. Another lyrical and significant melody is theme II B,[20] in the dominant key,

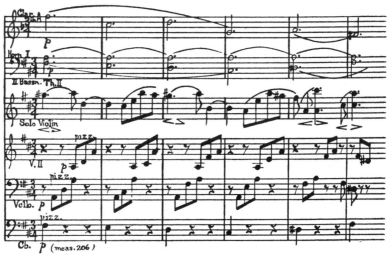

20. The employment of three themes in addition to a closing theme is unusual in the exposition of a sonata form.

comprising two long and expansive phrases (30 measures). The strong emphasis upon the inharmonic tone (*g-sharp*) is a characteristic trait in the work of Brahms.[21] Refractory intervals in the solo part

and similar technical difficulties in the concerto require a large and supple left-hand and a "blitzschnellende Treffsicherheit."

The development has six sections. Here Brahms exhibits his consummate mastery in the manipulation and assimilation of his thematic material. Both the solo violin and orchestra have vital roles. The beginning of the first section (meas. 272) coincides with the close of the solo exposition. Another version of motive N[3] is declaimed in the keys of A minor and C major. Section 2 (meas. 288) involves theme II B and figure *t*. In section 3 (meas. 304) the key of C minor is definitely established. There are agitated syncopes and complementary rhythms in the strings, forming the accompaniment of figure *t*:

Figure *t* is subsequently transferred to the wood-winds (meas. 312) and strings, while the solo violin pursues a delicate variation above it:

21. A similar example may be found in measure 172.

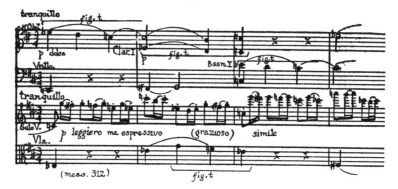

Section 4 (meas. 332) stands out in bold relief because of the energetic trills of the solo, abstracted from the first theme, and the imitative character of the orchestral part. The sextolet passages in measure 339 were the subject of controversy between Joachim and Brahms. Joachim suggested the following arpeggios to strengthen that measure:

Brahms, however, decided on these:

A passage from Section 5 is conspicuous because of its anacrustic rhythm, precipitous leaps, and wide range. It progresses in two-measure phrases:

Section 6 (meas. 361) begins in the dominant key and veers toward the tonic key in anticipation of the reprise. An iambic rhythm from the closing theme[22] and fragmentary material from the first theme are salient features.

The reprise (meas. 381) begins with a climactic presentation of theme I (flute, oboe, clarinet, and two horns), accompanied by a new counterpoint in the bassoons, violoncellos, and contrabasses. The reiteration of the material from the exposition is in accordance with the austere, formal structure of the movement. Theme II A (meas. 419) modulates to the tonic key in the course of its announcement, and theme II B (meas. 445) reappears in the mediant key (F-sharp major). The violin cadenza was left to the discretion of the soloist—a practice that was common in the time of Mozart and Beethoven. The original cadenza was written by Joachim. Later, however, others by Halir, Auer, Marteau, and Busoni were frequently used.

With the opening of the masterly coda (meas. 527), we discover some of the finest effects in the entire movement. The principal theme is transfigured melodically and harmonically, as the accompaniment moves for several measures in a chromatic succession of triads.

The profound Adagio is remarkable for its contrasts of mood, blending of motives, melodic figurations, rhythmic subtleties, striking modulations, and effective participation of the wind instruments. The form is ternary: A — A' — transition — B — A — coda. The theme (F major) is played by the oboe, and has the character of a pastoral folk song:

An embellished version of it is given to the solo violin (meas. 32), beginning section A'. The transition (meas. 46-56) reveals thematic figures in contrary motion,

22. See measures 361 and 78.

borrowed from measure 11, which are utilized for the chromatic modulation from C to G-flat major (meas. 45-48), and for the enharmonic modulation to B major (meas. 50-52). A diminution of these figures may be found in measures 54, 60-61, and 69-73.

We proceed to the remote key of F-sharp minor for the presentation of the second theme (meas. 56) and the contrasting middle section:

Its polyphonic setting recalls to us the texture of another idiomatic passage in this section:

After a few climactic measures, we are prepared for the tonic key
and the return of the theme with these coloristic harmonies:

Note especially the tonic pedal-point below an altered IV^7 chord
(meas. 76), and then a V^7, altered on the last pulse of the next
measure. Similar chordal combinations were used by Spohr and
Mendelssohn in their violin concertos.

The original melody returns in the oboe part (meas. 78), accompanied by new figurations in the solo violin. The melody is
shifted to the solo violin part in measures 80-82 as the embellished
version of measures 32-34 is suddenly interposed; but the original
melody is resumed by the oboe in measure 83. We observe that
measures 78-79 and 83-90 correspond with measures 3-4 and 7-14.
The coda (meas. 91) is consummately Romantic as the solo violin
part ascends to the upper registers, freely and dramatically elab-
orating motive K in the orchestra.

The rugged and virile finale, Allegro giocoso, ma non troppo
vivace, offers a dynamic contrast with the temper of the preceding movement. Its form is a large rondo with the following sub-
divisions:

Section A (meas. 1-35), with the main theme

First transition (meas. 35-57)

Section B (meas. 57-93), with the second theme beginning in
the dominant key

Section A (meas. 93-108), abbreviated

Second transition (meas. 108-119)

Section C (meas. 120-141), with a new theme beginning in the sub-dominant key

Third transition (meas. 141-150)

Section B (meas. 150-182), beginning in the sub-dominant key

Fourth transition (meas. 183-187)

Section A (meas. 187-222), rather fragmentary presentation

Episodical and transitional cadenza section (meas. 222-267)

Coda, beginning in measure 267

The first theme is conceived in the spirit of a Hungarian folk dance:

Motive Y is of fundamental importance throughout the movement. *Leggiero* violin passages in measures 43-48 are pitted against involved rhythmic combinations:

The second theme is pompous and defiant. Note especially measure 59 with its imitative thematic fragment in contrary motion:

After another pronouncement of the first theme, there is an obvious trend toward the sub-dominant key, and we are prepared for a new theme with strong anacrustic effects:

Recurrences of theme II and theme I are succeeded by a brief polyphonic episode with cumbrous double-stopping and conflicting linear effects:

Here Brahms ". . . toils in cyclopean workshops: mighty forces serve him; but they are sometimes refractory, and must be coerced by a strong and imperious will."[23]

The auspicious coda (Poco più presto) restates motives from the two main themes, and displays ingenious rhythmic effects. After four measures there is a sportive and humorous version of the first theme.[24]

This version is enhanced by grace-note flourishes in the woodwinds and first violins. Oppositional rhythms (meas. 339-342) and syncopations (meas. 333-336) near the close are conspicuous because of their independence and vitality.

23. P. Spitta, "Johannes Brahms," in *Zur Musik: Sechzehn Aufsätze*, p. 419.
24. See *supra*, p. 138.

SUMMARY

Although the Brahms Violin Concerto has a conservative instrumentation, the scoring is not conventional. The *Selbstherrlichkeit* of the individual instruments is an outstanding quality of the orchestral setting. The orchestral parts are closely interwoven with the solo, and are equally significant.[25] The soloist ". . . maintains his hereditary and inalienable right, but renounces his once absolute rule and satisfies himself with constitutional government. . . ."[26]

In review, we submit these stylistic features of the Brahms Violin Concerto:

> Symphonic conception
> Organic unity
> Masculine character
> Marked contrasts of mood
> Floridity
> Rhythmic vitality and subtlety (transcendence of metrical limitations by expressive rhythmical units and patterns; use of oppositional rhythms, anacrusis, and syncopation)
> Concentrative motive technique
> Contrapuntal textures
> Adroit modulations
> Vital conceptions of dissonance
> Use of pedal-point (see first movement, meas. 90-119; second movement, meas. 75-77; and third movement, meas. 255-265)

25. This is also true of the orchestration in Brahms' Concertos for Pianoforte and Orchestra, opera 15 and 83; and the Concerto for Violin, Violoncello, and Orchestra, opus 102.

26. Kalbeck, *Johannes Brahms*, Vol. III, p. 206.

CONCLUSION

I T HAS BEEN ADDUCED that the German Romanticists emulated the Classicists in the general plan of the violin concerto. A sonata form with a double exposition was adopted as the basic design of the first movement. Following the examples of Mozart and Beethoven, the composers frequently utilized a voluminous orchestral exposition in which the principal themes or thematic fragments were set forth in the tonic major or minor keys.[1] In the concertos with minor tonalities, however, a favorite procedure was to present the subordinate theme in the relative major key, as in the solo exposition. Examples of this may be observed in Spohr (Concertos Nos. II and VI), Schumann (Concerto in D minor), Ernst (Concerto, opus 23), and Joachim (Concerto, opus 11). As the German Romanticists evolved a greater freedom in the formal structure of the concerto, they evinced a tendency either to minimize the orchestral exposition or else to exclude it. Spohr, in Concertos Nos. XI and XII, used a brief and rather episodical orchestral exposition as an introduction. Bruch employed only an introductory motive in his Concerto, opus 26; and, like Mendelssohn before him, he omitted the orchestral exposition in the Concerto, opus 44. On the other hand, Brahms emulated Beethoven by using a long orchestral exposition (89 measures), which

1. See *supra*, pp. 5, 6.

contained much of the thematic substance of the first movement.

For the second movement, these composers gave preferential use to the ternary form with a coda.

In the construction of the third movement, the rondo was generally the standard design. It became more involved and less conventional as the era progressed.

Emphasis was given to the structure of the violin concerto as an organic whole by linking together some or all of the movements (Mendelssohn, Bruch), or by using the *principe cyclique* (Raff, Bruch, Sitt), or through the conception of works in one movement (Ernst, Goetz).

Other striking formal procedures include:

First Movement

Enlargement of the coda from a brief orchestral tutti to the status of a "second development" (Mendelssohn, Raff, Brahms)

Introduction of new themes in the development and coda

Use of free recitatives (Spohr, Bruch)

Cadenza written out by the composer (Spohr, Mendelssohn, Joachim, Reinecke, Goetz, Goldmark, Dietrich)

Elimination of the cadenza (Spohr, David, Schumann, Raff, Bruch, Damrosch, Rüfer)

Elimination of the reprise (Bruch)

Second Movement

Recitatives and free designs (Spohr, Bruch)

Variation form (Bohrer)

Third Movement

Relinquishment of the Alla polacca type

Employment of a scherzo as the concluding movement (Maurer)

Use of the sonata form (Raff, Bruch, Goldmark)

Use of irregular designs (Bruch)

HARMONY

Emphasis upon mediant and sub-mediant key relationships, following the examples of Schubert and Beethoven

Use of harmony as a coloristic medium involving chromaticism and enharmony (Spohr, Goldmark)

Mediaeval modes (Brüll)

Beginning of the transition from vertical harmonic concepts to a modern linear and horizontal technique. This transition was propelled by Mendelssohn, Bruch, and Goldmark, and culminated during the Romantic period in the work of Brahms

New concepts of dissonance

MELOS

Embellishments (Spohr, Mendelssohn, Bruch, Goldmark, Rüfer, Brahms)

Penetration of the folk tune into the violin concerto (Spohr, Maurer, Joachim), anteceding the nationalistic trend of later Romantic music

The employment of the motive as a vital melodic and formal unit (Molique, Mendelssohn, David, Bruch, Goldmark, Dietrich, Brahms)

Irregular phraseology

RHYTHM

Frequent use of syncopation

Anacrusis (Bruch, Brahms, Gernsheim)

Oppositional rhythms

Recurring metrical changes (Spohr, Goetz)

Conflict of rhythm and meter (Bruch, Brahms)

Employment of a basic rhythmic motive (Bruch)

VIOLIN TECHNIQUE

The commanding influence of Paganini succeeded that of the French virtuosi, Rode, Kreutzer, and Baillot. This pertained especially to:

Use of the entire range of the violin

Employment of varied and exceptional bowing styles, such as the *spiccato, sautillé, saltando, ricochet,* etc.

Amplification of double-stop technique

Development of *flageolet* technique

Development of the left-hand pizzicato

The accompanying orchestral apparatus was enlarged, resulting in the expansion of the brass choir so that it included four horns, two trumpets, and three trombones. Archaic instrumental parts, such as the clarino, employed by Spohr and other composers during the first half of the nineteenth century, became obsolete. On the other hand, the violoncello and the contrabass parts emerged separate and independent; and *divisi* effects were common. The significance of the orchestral accompaniment rose, until with Brahms it attained a position of virtually equal importance with the solo part. It is in this direction that composers of the twentieth century, notably Sibelius, Pfitzner, Hindemith, and others have advanced.

On the basis of the Romantic temperament, several divergent trends were evident. There were composers with a virtuosic bias (Paganini, Bohrer, Mayseder, Ernst); *verinnerlichte* writers (Spohr, Joachim); creators whose pianistic conceptions betrayed the fact that they wrote for an instrument with which they had little more than a theoretical acquaintance (Schumann, Raff, Goetz, Gernsheim, Rüfer); other composers with highly subjective and sensuous qualities (Goldmark and Bruch); and, finally, there was Brahms with a virile symphonic conception of the concerto.

In conclusion, as we view these phases of Romanticism, we recall that in the background of the musical evolution there was regnant the spirit of reform, democracy, and revolution. "Retour à la Nature!" was the cry of Rousseau. The philosophies of Kant,

Fichte, Schelling, Hegel, Schopenhauer, Nietzsche, and Marx; the poetry of Goethe, Schiller, Novalis, Tieck, Jean Paul, Grillparzer, Uhland, Rückert, Wordsworth, Coleridge, Byron, Keats, Shelley, Tennyson, and Browning; the novels and dramas of Scott, Dickens, Thackeray, Meredith, Flaubert, Zola, Gogol, Dostoievsky, Tolstoy, Ibsen, and Björnson; the art of the Pre-Raphaelites—all of these represent the various and manifold creeds of Romanticism.

With the new pre-eminence of the individual, it appears to us *as if the violin were that singular instrument through which the soul of Romanticism could best express itself.* It is no wonder, then, that the notable achievements in the development of violin playing and violin composition are among the imposing contributions of Romantic music.

APPENDICES

PUBLICATION DATES OF THE CONCERTOS REVIEWED[1]

Dates	Composers	Concertos
Prior to 1828	Böhm	No. I, in D major
	Bohrer	Nos. I, op. 9; IV, op. 27; V, op. 40
	Mayseder	Nos. I, op. 22; III, op. 28
	Kalliwoda	E major, op. 9
	Maurer	Nos. I, II, V, VI, VII
	Spohr	Nos. I-XI, op. 1, 2, 7, 10, 17, 28, 38, 47, 55, 62, 70
1828–1844	Lipinski	*Militaire,* op. 21
	Molique	No. V, op. 21
	Spohr	Nos. XII-XIV (published as Concertinos Nos. I, II, III), op. 79, 92, 110
1845	Mendelssohn	E minor, op. 64
1844–1851	Ernst	F-sharp minor, op. 23
	Spohr	No. XV, op. 128
1851	Paganini	Nos. I, op. 6; II, op. 7
1852–1859	David	No. V, op. 35
1860–1867	Joachim	*Hungarian,* op. 11
1868	Bruch	No. I, op. 26
1877	Bruch	No. II, op. 44
	Reinecke	No. II, op. 141
1878	Raff	No. II, op. 206
1874–1879	Dietrich	D minor, op. 30
	Goldmark	A minor, op. 28
	Hellmesberger, J.	Fragment of a Concerto in C major, begun by Beethoven
	Hiller	A major, op. 152
1879	Brahms	D major, op. 77
1880	Gernsheim	D major, op. 42
1883	Strauss	D minor, op. 8

1. C. F. Whistling, *Handbuch der musikalischen Literatur.* Leipzig: Whistling, 2. Auflage, 1828. For other editions and supplementary volumes, consult the bibliography.

T. Müller-Reuter, *Lexikon der deutschen Konzertliteratur,* Bd. I, and Nachtrag zu Bd. I.

Dates	Composers	Concertos
1880–1885	Brüll	A minor, op. 41
	Goetz	G major, op. 22
	Rüfer	D minor, op. 33
	Sitt	A minor, op. 21
1937	Schumann	D minor
Unpublished:	Mendelssohn	An early violin concerto
Unpublished:	Damrosch	Concerto in F-sharp minor

RECORDINGS OF THE CONCERTOS REVIEWED

BRAHMS

Concerto in D major, op. 77
Kreisler and the London Philharmonic Orchestra
    Victor records: Album M-402 (14588-14592-S)
                     Album AM-402 (14593-14596-S)
Heifetz and the Boston Symphony Orchestra
    Victor records: Album M-581 (15526-15530-S)
                     Album AM-581 (15531-15535-S)
Szigeti and the Halle Orchestra
    Columbia records: Set no. 117 (10 parts)

BRUCH

Concerto No. I in G minor, op. 26
Menuhin and the London Symphony Orchestra
    Victor records: Album M-124 (7509-7511)
                     Album AM-124 (7512-7514)
Campoli and a Symphony Orchestra under the direction of W. Goehr
    Columbia records: Set M-332 (69243-D—69245-D)
                   Set AM-332 (69246-D—69248-D)
  Second movement (Adagio)
  Kulenkampf and the Berlin Philharmonic Orchestra
    T-E1492

GOLDMARK

Concerto in A minor, op. 28
Second movement (Air, Andante)
Morini, with pianoforte accompaniment
  G-EJ 237

MENDELSSOHN

Concerto in E minor, op. 64
Kreisler and the London Philharmonic Orchestra
    Victor records: Album M-277 (8786-8788)
                     Album AM-277 (8789-8791)
Szigeti and the London Philharmonic Orchestra
    Columbia records: Set 190 (8 parts)

PAGANINI

Concerto in D major, op. 6
Menuhin and the Paris Symphony Orchestra
Victor records: Album M-230 (8379-8383)
Album AM-230 (8384-8388)
Concerto in D major (first movement) transcribed by Kreisler
Kreisler and the Philadelphia Symphony Orchestra
Victor records: Album M-361 (14420-14421)

SCHUMANN

Concerto in D minor
Menuhin and the New York Philharmonic-Symphony Orchestra
Victor records: Album M-451 (14913-14916-S)
Album AM-451 (14917-14920-S)

SPOHR

Concerto No. VIII in A minor, op. 47 (*In Form einer Gesangsszene*)
Kulenkampf and the Berlin Philharmonic Orchestra
Telefunken E 1847-1849
Spalding and the Philadelphia Orchestra
V-M 544

SUPPLEMENTARY LIST OF COMPOSERS

Other composers whose violin concertos may be considered within the scope of German Romanticism include:

Kummer, G. H.	1774-1857	Gerke, O.	1807-1878
Clement, F.	1780-1842	Rietz, J.	1812-1877
Kähler, M. F. A.	1781-1834	Hennig, K. G.	1819-1873
Matthäi, H.	1781-1835	Uhlig, T.	1822-1853
Henning, C. G.	1784-1867	Wüerst, R.	1824-1881
Eberwein, C.	1786-1868	Müller, B. A. G.	1824-1883
Guhr, K. W. F.	1787-1848	Reissmann, A.	1825-1903
Lindpainter, P. J.	1791-1856	Bott, J. J.	1826-1895
Täglichsbeck, T.	1799-1867	Urban, H.	1837-1901
Hellmesberger, G.	1800-1873	Becker, R.	1842-1924
Ries, H.	1802-1886	Struss, F.	1847- ?
Pott, A.	1806-1883	Carl, M.	1847-1906

Various authors, Riemann, Engel, and Emery, for example, cite the names of other German composers who ostensibly wrote violin concertos during this period:

André, J. A.	1775-1860	Dörstling, G.	1821- ?
Hofmeister, F.	1782-1864	Witting, K.	1823-1907
Abel, A.	1783- ?	Hüllweck, F.	1824-1887
Ries, F.	1784-1838	Seifriz, M.	1827-1885
Weber, C. M. von	1786-1826	Hohnstock, C.	1828-1889
Steinmetz, N. W.	1793- ?	Spies, E.	1830- ?
Jansa, L.	1795-1875	Abel, L.	1834-1895
Grünberg, G.	1802- ?	Draeseke, F. A. B.	1835-1913
Wichtl, G.	1805-1877	Blumenstengel, A.	1835-1895
Hermann, G.	1808-1878	Zenger, M.	1837-1911
Titl, A. E.	1809-1882	Fritze, W.	1842-1881
Fischel, A(?).	1810- ?	Grammann, K.	1842-1897
Wolff, H.	1813-1898	Venzl, J.	1842-1916
Dont, J.	1815-1888	Ludwig, F.	1846-1913
Engel, K.	1818-1882	Krug, A.	1849-1904
Köttlitz, A.	1820-1860		

PUBLICATION DATES AND PUBLISHERS OF CONCERTOS BY COMPOSERS IN THE SUPPLEMENTARY LIST[1]

Dates	Composers	Concertos	Publishers
1809	Matthäi, H.	E major, op. 2	Kühnel
1819		No. II, in G major, op. 9	Hofmeister
1820	Kummer, G. H.	*très facile,* op. 20	
1822	Matthäi, H.	No. III, op. 15	Peters
1824	Henning, C. G.	D minor, op. 15	André
1827	Eberwein, C.	*Dilletanten-Concert,* op. 40	Hofmeister
1828	Clement, F.	No. I	Haslinger
		No. II	
	Kähler, M. F. A.	No. I, in E major	Breitkopf & Härtel
	Matthäi, H.	No. IV, op. 20	Hofmeister
1829–1833	Guhr, K. W. F.	No. I, in E major, op. 15 *(Le Souvenir de Paganini)*	Schott
	Pott, A.	A minor, op. 10 *(Les Adieux de Copen-hague)*	Hofmeister
		D minor, op. 15	Kistner
Prior to 1844	Hellmesberger, G.	No. I, op. 12	Diabelli
	Hennig, K.	A major	Gombart
	Lindpainter, P. J.	op. 42	Kistner
	Ries, H.	D major, op. 13	Bote & Bock
		A minor, op. 16	
	Täglichsbeck, T.	*Militaire,* in D major, op. 8	Hofmeister
1844–1847	Gerke, O.	No. I, in E minor, op. 28	Breitkopf & Härtel

1. See p. 153. The concertos by Matthäi, Struss, and Urban are available at the Library of Congress.

In addition to the sources given on p. 149, the author referred to [C. F. Whistling] *Handbuch der musikalischen Litteratur oder allgemeines systematisch geordenetes Verzeichniss der bis zum Ende des Jahres 1815 gedruckten Musikalien,*

Dates	Composers	Concertos	Publishers
1852–1859	Müller, B. A. G.	No. I, in D major, op. 2	Spehr
	Rietz, J.	G major, op. 30	Kistner
1860	Bott, J. J.	A major, op. 21	Peters
1860–1873	Wüerst, R.	A major, op. 37	Peters
1874–1879	Becker, R.	op. 4	Hoffarth
	Reissmann, A.	op. 30	Bote & Bock
	Urban, H.	D minor, op. 22	Challier
1883	Carl, M.	E major	Bellmann & Thümer
	Struss, F.	No. I, in A minor, op. 4	Kistner

auch musikalischen Schriften und Abbildungen mit Anzeige der Verleger und Preise (Leipzig: A. Meysel, 1817). Supplements to the above volume were also issued between 1818 and 1827.

BIBLIOGRAPHY

BIBLIOGRAPHY

ABER, ADOLF. *Handbuch der Musikliteratur*. Leipzig: Breitkopf und Härtel, 1922.

ADLER, GUIDO. *Der Stil in der Musik* (1. Buch). Leipzig: Breitkopf und Härtel, 1911.

ADLER, GUIDO (Herausgeber). *Handbuch der Musikgeschichte*. Frankfurt am Main: Frankfurter Verlags-Anstalt A. G., 1924.

AMBROS, AUGUST W. *Culturhistorische Bilder aus dem Musikleben der Gegenwart*. Leipzig: H. Matthes, 2. Auflage, 1865.

BAGGE, S. "Die geschichtliche Entwicklung der Sonate," *Sammlung musikalischer Vorträge,* herausgegeben von Paul Graf Waldersee, Bd. II. Leipzig: Breitkopf und Härtel, 1880.

BAILLOT, PIERRE. *L'Art du Violon*. Berlin: Schlesinger.

BATKA, R., and NAGEL, W. *Allgemeine Geschichte der Musik*. Bd. III. Stuttgart: Grüninger.

BERLIOZ, HECTOR. *Mémoires*. Paris: M. Levy Frères, 1870.

BERNSDORF, E. (Herausgeber). *Neues Universal-Lexikon der Tonkunst.* 3 Bde., 1856, 1857, 1861; erster Nachtrag, 1865.

BRACHARZ, L. *Die Solovioline bei Beethoven*. Dissertation, University of Vienna, 1929.

BRENET, MICHEL. *Dictionnaire Pratique et Historique de la Musique*. Paris: Colin, 1926.

BÜCKEN, ERNST. *Die Musik des 19. Jahrhunderts bis zur Moderne*. Handbuch der Musikwissenschaft, herausgegeben von E. Bücken. Wildpark-Potsdam: Akademische Verlagsgesellschaft, Athenaion m. b. H., 1929.

COLLES, H. C. *Brahms*. New York: Brentano's, 1908.

DEITERS, HERMANN. "Brahms," *Sammlung musikalischer Vorträge,* herausgegeben von Paul Graf Waldersee, II. Teil. Leipzig: Breitkopf und Härtel, 1898.

ECKARDT, JULIUS. *Ferdinand David und die Familie Mendelssohn-Bartholdy*. Leipzig: Duncker und Humblot, 1888.

EITNER, ROBERT. *Biographisch-bibliographisches Quellen-Lexikon*. Leipzig: Breitkopf und Härtel, 1903.

EMERY, F. B. *The Violin Concerto*. Chicago: The Violin Literature Publishing Co., 1928.

Engel, Hans. *Das Instrumentalkonzert,* Führer durch den Konzertsaal, begonnen von H. Kretzschmar (*Die Orchestermusik,* Bd. III). Leipzig: Breitkopf und Härtel, 1932.

Enyedi, Georg. *Studien zur Psychologie der Wiederholung in der Musik.* Dissertation, University of Vienna, 1930.

Fétis, F. J. *Biographie Universelle des Musiciens,* Vol. VI. Paris: Didot Frères, Fils et Cie., deuxième édition, 1884.

Fuller-Maitland, J. A. *Brahms.* New York: J. Lane Co., 1911.

Glöckner, Ernst. *Studien zur romantischen Psychologie der Musik.* Dissertation, University of Munich, 1909.

Grove, George. *Grove's Dictionary of Music and Musicians,* edited by H. C. Colles. New York: Macmillan Co., 3rd edition, 1935.

Haas, Robert M. *Aufführungspraxis der Musik.* Handbuch der Musikwissenschaft, herausgegeben von E. Bücken. Wildpark-Potsdam: Akademische Verlagsgesellschaft, Athenaion m. b. H., [1933].

Hadow, W. H. *Studies in Modern Music.* New York: Macmillan Co., 12th edition, second series, 1923.

Hanslick, Eduard. *Aus meinem Leben.* Berlin: 3. Auflage, 1894.

————. *Concerte, Componisten und Virtuosen der letzten fünfzehn Jahre: 1870-1885.* Berlin: Allgemein Verein für deutsche Literatur, 1886.

————. *Geschichte des Concertwesens in Wien.* Wien: W. Braumüller, 1869.

————. *Vom musikalischen Schönen.* Leipzig: J. A. Barth, 7. Auflage, 1885.

Hartmann, Arthur. "The Brahms Violin Concerto," *Musical Courier,* Vol. XIII, No. I. New York: 1916.

Heuberger, R. *Musikalische Skizzen.* Leipzig: H. Seemann Nachfolger, 1901.

Jadassohn, S. *Wesen der Melodie.* Leipzig: Breitkopf und Härtel, 1899.

Jenner, Gustav. *Johannes Brahms als Mensch, Lehrer und Künstler.* Marburg: N. G. Elwert, 2. Auflage, 1930.

Joachim, J., and Moser, A. *Violinschule.* Berlin and Leipzig: Simrock G. m. b. H. [1905].

Kalbeck, M. *Johannes Brahms.* Bd. I, Wiener Verlag, 1904; II. and III. Bde., Verlag der Deutschen Brahms-Gesellschaft, 1908, 1910.

Knepler, Georg. *Die Form in den Instrumentalwerken Johannes Brahms'.* Dissertation, University of Vienna, 1930.

Krause, Emil. *Brahms.* Hamburg: Gräfe und Sillem, 1892.

Kurth, Ernst. *Die romantische Harmonik.* Berlin: Max Hesse Verlag, 3. Auflage, 1923.

Lach, Robert W. *Das Konstruktionsprinzip der Wiederholung in Musik, Sprache und Literatur.* Wien: Hölder-Pichler-Tempsky A. G., 1925.

La Mara (Lipsius, Ida M.). "Brahms," *Musikalische Studienköpfe.* Leipzig: H. Schmidt und C. Günther, Bd. III, 4. Auflage, 1878.

————. "David," *Musikalische Studienköpfe*. Bd. III, 4. Auflage, 1878.

————. "Felix Mendelssohn-Bartholdy," *Musikalische Studienköpfe*. Bd. I, 5. Auflage, 1879.

LAMPADIUS, W. A. *Felix Mendelssohn-Bartholdy: Ein Gesamtbild seines Lebens und Wirkens*. Leipzig: F. Leuckart, 1886.

LITZMANN, BERTHOLD. *Clara Schumann*. Leipzig: Breitkopf und Härtel, 1905.

———— (Herausgeber). *Clara Schumann—Johannes Brahms Briefe*. Leipzig: Breitkopf und Härtel, Bd. II, 1927.

MALIBRAN, ALEXANDER. *Louis Spohr: Sein Leben und Wirken*. Frankfurt am Main: Sauerlände, 1860.

MARX, A. B. *Die Musik des 19. Jahrhunderts und ihre Pflege*. Leipzig: Breitkopf und Härtel, 1855.

MENDELSSOHN-BARTHOLDY, JAKOB LUDWIG FELIX. *Briefe aus den Jahren 1830 bis 1847*. Leipzig: H. Mendelssohn, 2 Bde., 1863-1864. Bd. I: *Reisebriefe aus den Jahren 1830 bis 1832*, herausgegeben von Paul Mendelssohn-Bartholdy, 5. Auflage. Bd. II: *Briefe aus den Jahren 1833 bis 1847*, herausgegeben von Paul Mendelssohn-Bartholdy und Carl Mendelssohn-Bartholdy, 2. Auflage.

MOSER, ANDREAS (Herausgeber). *Johannes Brahms im Briefwechsel mit Joseph Joachim*. Berlin: Verlag der Deutschen Brahms-Gesellschaft, 2 Bde., 1908.

————. *Joseph Joachim: Ein Lebensbild*. Verlag der Deutschen Brahms-Gesellschaft, 2 Bde., 1908.

MOSER, H. J. *Geschichte der deutschen Musik vom Auftreten Beethovens bis zur Gegenwart*. Stuttgart and Berlin: J. G. Cotta'sche Buchhandlung Nachfolger, 1924.

MOZART, LEOPOLD. *Violinschule*. Wien: C. Stephenson, 1922.

MÜLLER-REUTER, THEODOR. *Lexikon der deutschen Konzertliteratur*. Leipzig: Kahnt Nachfolger; Bd. I, 1909; Nachtrag zu Bd. I, 1921.

NAGEL, WILLIBALD. "Über das Romantische in der deutschen Musik," *Jahrbuch Peters*, 12. Jahrgang, 1905. Leipzig: Peters.

NEDWED, WOLFGANG. *Die Entwicklung der Instrumentation von der Wiener Klassik bis zu den Anfängen Richard Wagners*. Dissertation, University of Vienna, 1931.

NEURATH, G. H. *Das Geigenkonzert der Wiener Klassiker*. Dissertation, University of Vienna, 1926.

NIEMANN, WALTER. *Brahms*. Berlin: Schuster und Loeffler, 1. bis 10. Auflage, 1920.

NIGGLI, A. "Nicolo Paganini," *Sammlung musikalischer Vorträge,* herausgegeben von Paul Graf Waldersee, Bd. IV. Leipzig: Breitkopf und Härtel, 1882.

NOHL, LUDWIG. *Spohr*. Musiker-Biographien, Bd. VII. Leipzig: P. Reclam jun., 1883?

PAZDIREK, FRANZ. *Universal Handbuch der Musikliteratur aller Zeiten und Völker*. Wien: Pazdirek, 1904.

PROUT, EBENEZER. "On the Growth of the Modern Orchestra during the Past Century," *Proceedings of the Musical Association*, Session V, 1878-1879. London: Stanley, Lucas & Weber, 1879.

REIMANN, HEINRICH. *Johannes Brahms*. Berühmte Musiker, herausgegeben von H. Reimann. Berlin: Verlagsgesellschaft für Literatur und Kunst, 1898.

REINECKE, KARL. "Mendelssohn," *Meister der Tonkunst*. Berlin and Stuttgart: W. Spemann, 1903.

REISSMANN, AUGUST. *Felix Mendelssohn-Bartholdy: Sein Leben und seine Werke*. Berlin: J. Guttentag, 2. Auflage, 1872.

RIEMANN, HUGO. *Geschichte der Musik seit Beethoven*. Berlin and Stuttgart: W. Spemann, 1901.

————. *Musiklexikon*, bearbeitet von A. Einstein. Berlin: M. Hesse, 11. Auflage, 1929.

ROCKSTRO, W. S. *Mendelssohn*. London: S. Low, Marston and Co. Ltd., 5th edition.

SACHS, C. *Real-Lexikon der Musikinstrumente*. Berlin: J. Bard, 1913.

SCHENKER, H. *Das Meisterwerk in der Musik*. München, Wien, Berlin: Drei Masken Verlag A. G., Bd. II, 1926.

SCHERING, ARNOLD. *Geschichte des Instrumentalkonzerts bis auf die Gegenwart*. Leipzig: Breitkopf und Härtel, 1905; 2. Auflage, 1927.

SCHLETTERER, H. M. "Louis Spohr," *Sammlung musikalischer Vorträge*, herausgegeben von Paul Graf Waldersee, Bd. III. Leipzig: Breitkopf und Härtel, 1881.

SCHOTTKY, J. M. *Paganini's Leben und Treiben*. Prag: J. G. Calve'sche Buchhandlung, 1830.

SCHRADER, BRUNO. *Mendelssohn*. Musiker-Biographien, Bd. XXI. Leipzig: P. Reclam jun., 1897.

SCHRÖDER, F. *Bernhard Molique und seine Instrumentalkompositionen*. Stuttgart: Verlag Berthold und Schwerdtner, 1923.

SCHUMANN, ROBERT. *Gesammelte Schriften über Musik und Musiker*, Bd. III. Leipzig: 1854; 2. Auflage, Bd. II, 1871.

————. "Neue Bahnen," *Neue Zeitschrift für Musik*, Bd. XXXIX.

SCHWERS, P., and FRIEDLAND, M. *Das Konzertbuch*. Bd. II: *Instrumental-Solokonzerte*. Stuttgart: Mut'sche Verlagsbuchhandlung, 1931.

SITTARD, JOSEF. "Felix Mendelssohn-Bartholdy," *Sammlung musikalischer Vorträge*, herausgegeben von Paul Graf Waldersee, Bd. III. Leipzig: Breitkopf und Härtel, 1881.

SPITTA, PHILIPP. "Johannes Brahms," *Zur Musik: Sechzehn Aufsätze*. Berlin: Paetel, 1892.

SPOHR, LOUIS. *Selbstbiographie*. Kassel and Göttingen: G. H. Wigand, 2 Bde., 1860-1861.

————. *Violinschule*. Wien: Haslinger, Originalausgabe, 1832.

STOEVING, PAUL. *Von der Violine*. Berlin-Grosslichterfelde: F. Vieweg G. m. b. H., 1906.

STÖHR, RICHARD. *Musikalische Formenlehre*. Leipzig: C. F. W. Siegel (R. Linnemann).

URBANTSCHITSCH, V. *Die Entwicklung der Sonatenform bei Brahms*. Festschrift den Mitgliedern des Musikhistorischen Kongresses. Wien: Universal Edition, 1927.

WASIELIEWSKI, W. J. *Aus siebzig Jahren*. Stuttgart and Leipzig: Deutsche Verlags-Anstalt, 1897.

————. *Die Violine und ihre Meister*. Leipzig: Breitkopf und Härtel, 3. Auflage, 1893.

[WHISTLING, C. F.] Anon. *Handbuch der musikalischen Litteratur oder allgemeines systematisch geordenetes Verzeichniss der bis zum Ende des Jahres 1815 gedruckten Musikalien, auch musikalischen Schriften und Abbildungen mit Anzeige der Verleger und Preise*. Leipzig: A. Meysel, 1817. (Ten *Nachträge* were issued between 1818 and 1827.)

WHISTLING, C. F. *Handbuch der musikalischen Literatur*. Leipzig: Whistling, 2. Auflage, 1828.

(For information on subsequent editions and supplementary volumes by C. F. Whistling, A. Hofmeister, and F. Hofmeister, consult the article on "Whistling," in *Grove's Dictionary of Music and Musicians*, 3rd edition, 1935, Vol. V, p. 707.)

WILLIAMS, C. A. "The Rondo Form," *Proceedings of the Musical Association*, Session XVII. London: Novello, Ewer & Co., 1891.

WOLFF, ERNST. *Felix Mendelssohn-Bartholdy*. Berlin: Harmonie Verlagsgesellschaft für Literatur und Kunst, 1906.

INDEX

INDEX

167